ACKNOWLEDGEMENTS

As this book is approaching publication, I must thank people for their valued help in many ways.

Jennifer, who first read the one and only draft trying to make sense of it, then the tremendous offer by Jill Dixon-Carter to get it onto computer. This has been a mammoth task, for which I am extremely grateful. Bob Dixon-Carter is about to get it all on disc, a mystery to me, so again thank you Bob. Also to William who has been a great help.

Mike Pratt has been a big help in taking two new photos of the village from the 'cottage' end.

My daughter Maureen and her daughter Sarah have helped a lot with proof reading, and like the rest of my family given encouragement.

Now it will be in the hands of Post Haste in Pocklington, before becoming a book, which is mostly "just about me" and hopefully may interest readers.

P.S.

Sadly Irene died on 24th October 2007 before this book was finally in print. She had approved the layout and sorted out all the photographs. She would have hated to have had a long illness so we can only be greatful that her time in hospital was so short. All her many friends and family will miss her enormously, but one of her oldest friends quoted words of comfort she had once recieved, "she left her life behind her".

John Dewsbury (Jack) Megginson married Irene Oxtoby 1940

Jack Megginson died 1997

Anthony Dewsbury (Tony) Born 1943. married Pam Bell Children – Jane 　　　　　　Mark Jane married Richard (Curly) Cartledge Children – Laura 　　　　　　Edward Mark married Kate Andrews Divorced. Engaged to Lisa Coates	Jennifer Christine Born 1944. married Derek Rivis Children – Sally 　　　　　　Rebecca Adopted Michelle Divorced from Derek Married William Foster after death of Barbara. William's children – Richard 　　　　　　　　　　　Simon 　　　　　　　　　　　Katy Sally married Mike Dodgson Children – Christopher 　　　　　　Nicola Divorced. Married Jeff Whorley Child – Rachel Rebecca married Geoff Mort Child – Sophie	Maureen Born 1946. Married David Metcalfe Children – Lucy 　　　　　　Alison 　　　　　　Sarah Divorced from David Met her partner Barry Lonsdale. Lucy married Paul Longstaff. Divorced Married Colin Lefley Children – Hannah 　　　　　　Freya Alison's partner Duncan Rayson died Alison with partner Des Radcliffe. Child – Jack Desmond Sarah married Colin's brother Dave Lefley. Children – Samuel 　　　　　　Luke	Pamela Rachel Born 1947. Married Norman Webb Child – Ian Rachel died 1991. Norman died 1998.

NEWLAND PARK

It seems like yesterday as I see myself aged four in a sunny garden surrounding a large bungalow in Hull. A rather stocky little girl, with a mane of brown curls, and sturdy legs.

Before that, I can't remember the Victorian house in Dover Street where I spent the first four years, but I was told that snow was falling on March 9th 1919, when I was born. Also I heard I was carried out in the snow when two days old - so perhaps that explains why I have always loved snow.

I had a loud cry and cried often as a baby and the loud voice is still with me!

My mother was "getting on a bit" when I was born and hadn't been married long to my father, Frederick Harvey Hayes Oxtoby, a "fish, game and poultry dealer" who had a shop in Waterworks Street in the centre of Hull.

Mother, like many parents in those days seldom talked about her past. She had been born in London, moved to Birmingham, had married someone called Andrews, and had three daughters Ethel, Alice (always Lallie after I arrived and tried to pronounce the name) and Olive.

At some stage Mr Andrews departed to Australia, for what reason I never found out, leaving my mother to fend for herself and three girls. They had mysteriously moved to Hull by then, and apparently Mother had jobs in shops, I think, as baby-minders were cheap and easy to come by!

In her old age Lallie, looking back, spoke of being devastated to lose her Daddy and how one particular minder used to shut them in a dark cupboard if naughty.

Ethel died aged 15 in Hull Infirmary of peritonitis. By all accounts a beautiful girl whose early death nearly broke my mother's heart.

Mother seldom spoke of Ethel to me, but I heard of her "glowing happy face" after a visit to Hull Fair and how dreadful the funeral was on a pouring wet day. After that Mother favoured cremations.

An old family friend from Birmingham days visited us in his last years and told me how lovely and lively Alice was and how well she played the piano and sang, but she never played after losing Ethel.

Lallie was eighteen when I was born and suffered from taking me out in the pram as I yelled so much she had to "tip kids in the street" to push the pram while she carried me home!

We had Lizzie as a 'Mother's Help' and she lived in. She must have more or less taken me over, at least at night, as she kept me quiet with constant supplies of 'gripe water'. So much so that in the family it was known as "more" because I shouted loudly for it! Did I talk early, I know

I walked unaided at nine months, how old was I when weaned from this calming medicine?

Olive was nine at this time; my Father was always "at the shop" but must have been pleased to have a baby girl, as he pressed a five pound note into my tiny fingers! A fiver in those days was large, white and so rare, one signed on the back when paying with it!

Lallie always had boyfriends, and one at that time who had literary interests, got Lallie interested in good books, and gave her a small leather bound set of Shakespeare which had belonged to his father. I now treasure them myself.

Well – the move to 'Newland Park' was before my memory, but the five years we were there were very happy for all of us. The bungalow built in the New Zealand style and called "OIMARA" which I was told was Maori for welcome, had a veranda on two sides – on to which French windows and other windows opened. The hall with a parquet floor was long and wide, with sitting room (called drawing room), dining room with sitting space and four bedrooms having doors on either side. Another bedroom, which I shared with Olive, was further back near a box room and kitchen with scullery behind.

To one side at the back of the hall a little passage led to a very cold bathroom with separate toilet next to it and a door into the gravel yard.

Unlike to-day's 'posh' houses you will note there was one loo in a five-bedroom house. We used chamber pots still, and there were jugs and bowls in some bedrooms with "wash stands" which were always part of a bedroom 'suite' until around 1930.

The walls throughout the bungalow were 'colour washed' with 'distemper' in pale colours, and kitchens and bathrooms done in gloss paint. The dining room, much the most used, had a panel effect on walls with strips of dark wood. Patterned carpets and curtains mostly, but the drawing room had plain white cotton at the window – a large bay – decorated with wide bands of crochet "insertion". In there was a "modern" three-piece suite, very squashy and large, covered in blue grey thick cotton.

I never remember sitting in that room, but can see the dining room clearly with peacock blue velvet "chesterfield" (one end let down to make it suitable to lie on) and two wing-back matching chairs.

The mahogany dining table could be extended by a winding handle, and was often covered with a richly patterned chenille cloth; when a spill happened on the white 'double damask' used for all meals – a plate would be hurriedly placed under the white cloth to prevent coloured stains coming through from the chenille under cover.

There was also a huge, high mahogany sideboard – heavily carved and with four mirrors and ornate shelves. As I write it is still at Cot Nab today and the dining table is also in family use with its tall backed matching chairs.

When I was little the Dresden china ornaments stood proudly on the sideboard – resplendent with cherubs, garlands, wonderfully coloured flowers, and a surfeit of gilt! These ornaments consisted of three separate pieces – a base with splayed feet, central heart shaped section with a crown-like top piece added – all impressive if one liked that sort of thing!

I was always warned at children's parties "Be careful of the ornaments and don't hide the thimble near them".

These precious, rather ostentatious objects were sold when we left the bungalow and I'm sure fetched a minute fraction of what they would be valued at today. The deep blue china vases from the upper shelves survive to this day, if slightly damaged.

Lizzie, became "Lill" over the years, so I will use that name from now. She was an ardent worker 'as strong as a horse' – and polished the wood block hall floor frequently on hands and knees. Often I was astride her back, with her apron strings as reins! Lill often sang vigorously as she worked, mostly "Sally Army" hymns – as at some date in her rather obscure past she had been associated with the Salvation Army. "Onward Christian Soldiers" was a favourite.

I gather it was a case of too many children in one family, as she was sent from Shipley to Hull to be brought up by her aunt and uncle called Thompson in Arlington Street near the railway where Mr Thompson was a platelayer. His wife Minni sewed shirts at home for poor pay and they had two daughters Ethel and Gladys. There was a "son" called Bill also, but I was the mother of three children before Lallie told me that Bill belonged to Lill and had been the result of a brief encounter with a lodger! Even all those years later, and after Bill's death in his twenties, it was still a "secret"!

To return to Newland Park! While most families in that district had proper maids in uniform and perhaps "help with the rough" also, Lill cleaned everything well, cooked for the family and coped with "the rough" too.

My mother helped in many ways, but mostly out of doors with the poultry she reared for "the shop" - eggs, hens, ducks (on the drain which flowed along one side of the large garden and out under a bridge on Cottingham Road) a few turkeys and two goats.

Lill seemed to look after the goats, milking them and the milk was mostly sold to customers nearby for 'invalids'. Why we had goats I never knew, but they lived in the paddock beyond the garden, where Mary Allison next door kept a shaggy pony. To my joy, I was sometimes given a ride, but mostly galloped round the garden astride a sweeping brush! I had an imaginary friend before school days called Dorothy Chester and had long conversations with her and sometimes with a clipped box bush I considered a person!

Mother helped Lill on the big job of Mondays wash. I was considered too much of a nuisance when such work went on, so Ethel Thompson came across Hull on two trams to collect me, to spend the day in Arlington Street. Gladys had a job in a shoe shop and Bill, when not ill as he frequently was, worked on the railway.

I don't remember much about the Arlington Street house other than one went through a bedroom to reach the bathroom. Also that a beaded curtain hung across the hallway and at one time an old lady sat all day in the front room. Another lodger I expect.

My mother was quick to buy household gadgets and we had electrical equipment with dodgy sockets and flexes trailing around. An early vacuum cleaner – I remember the name "Tellus" on the handle was considered wonderful, as was the crystal set wireless, soon followed by one where the sound came through a large horn, so earphones were not needed.

We always had a telephone "7770", ours was the more modern type with receiver lifting off the bracket, but most in use were the pedestal ones with ear piece attached by a cord.

I've described the garden (where "Moody" came part time to work) in my "Mud" book, and all the antics I got up to with friends swinging and climbing or fishing for tiddlers in the drain.

My sisters had a little boat and it was a treat to go off in that. If going under Cottingham Road one had to lie flat!

I went to the French Convent aged five, along with Olive and soon made friends there who still remember that playground of a garden.

I've also already written of "Westbrook" the more grand house where the Fords lived in some style! A proper maid and a char. A morning room as well as dining and drawing rooms and the most grand W.C. I've ever seen! Shaped like a huge and imposing basket chair with arm rests! It did seem large to a four year old when I first went to play with Jacky Ford! A great companion of early years, and since his sister Enid read the "Mud" book we got in touch again when he was an elderly dentist in Rickmansworth. Even this week we have had phone conversations after the death of Enid.

I'm told, or was told as there is no one left who remembers, that I was a show-off little girl who embarrassed my sisters' boyfriends by my antics of turning somersaults or other knicker showing activities calling "Look at me! Look at me!" I think I got over some of that exhibitionism on going to school, but have always indulged in "showing off" if the opportunity arises. In old age I've enjoyed giving talks or readings.

Lallie led quite a social life at Newland Park and played a lot of tennis and bridge. She was a "Charleston" expert and the first to have "shingled" hair. A short style popular in the 20's. Even Mother and Lill lost their long hairstyles. I can still see Mother with a pretty hairstyle – rather piled up over a pad, before succumbing to 'bobs' and 'permanent waves'.

Hair was usually washed at home (Lill did mine until I was 18) and a slogan of the time was 'Friday night is Armami night' – popular shampoo – advertised on the billboards displayed in the town.

Clothes were washed on a weekly basis, yes – even knickers! Later when Lux was invented the frequent washing of "undies" became more the thing, with an advert proclaiming, "I'm a daily dipper are you?"

My mother was a constant washer of hair brushes and combs in Scrubbs ammonia – perhaps this went back to the troubles in the old days with nits. We had home remedies like syrup of figs for constipation, borasic powder for eyes, olive oil warmed for earache, soda water after a "bilious attack' and camphorated oil on the chest for colds.

One always had eucalyptus oil to sprinkle on hankies in the winter and lanolin for chapped skin. Plenty of that needed, in cold weather and short socks.

A doctor would call if needed. I only had a few childhood illnesses and escaped measles, mumps and whooping cough, though was once in bed with what the doctor called "Scarletina" and twice suffered from an abscess or boils.

I think I was four when a baby sister appeared. Children were not told of pregnancies; in fact such a condition was considered a rather secret and personal state. My mother had a nurse midwife and I suppose a doctor came, but I knew nothing of the danger to Mother's life when she developed a serious infection –septicaemia – but perhaps because of her strong character she thankfully recovered. No antibiotics.

This was again a great sadness when the pretty dark haired Joanie died aged two of pneumonia. Strange to record, I remember little of this wee sister, other than watching her being bathed in front of the kitchen fire. After her death she was laid out on the settee in the drawing room with curtains drawn, but I must have been whisked away for the funeral, perhaps to the Thompsons.

We were not a church going family then, but St. John's Newland was sometimes visited for Matins services and prayer books were kept in the drawer of the rather elaborate satinwood hall table with a matching chair on either side.

Our neighbours, the Alisons, were professional people and Mrs Alison a keen Christian Scientist who got my mother interested in going to the church on Beverley Road. She said later on, it was the beautiful readings from the bible that appealed to her.

This was the start of a lifelong membership of this church for mother and for Lill who read their "daily lessons" from Mary Baker Eddy's manual without fail for the rest of their lives. Some of this rubbed off on me, but as a schoolgirl I had no desire to take part in anything different from my friends and never admitted to any involvement! Incidentally Mr Alison sold us the old oak chest, which is still in my cottage hall. A son of the Alison's became an eminent surgeon in Leeds. Mary Alison became a doctor too, so the Christian Science belief didn't extend to all the family.

My father never went to any church as far as I knew. He had no education after the age of nine when he became an errand boy – so all credit to his hard work and later pride in being a partner in "Oxtoby and Johnson". I think it was something to do with dishonesty on Johnson's part why the business suffered a set back financially.

My father had an artistic streak in setting up wonderful and picturesque displays for passers-by in Waterworks Street. Fish, game and poultry set out on ice, or in the case of birds and hares, hanging from hooks in all the glory of feathers or fur.

I wish now I had kept photographs of the displays, but they disappeared in many moves. Naturally we lived on all the best fish, crab, lobster and game.

Sometimes on Thursdays (half-day closing) father joined us on outings to the countryside in the car, which was driven by Lallie, or my mother. He needed frequent stops at favourite pubs on route, but ladies remained in the car! "Just time for a quick one!"

He was a jolly man and always kind and generous, but not a "Daddy" type to be involved in any of my interests. He loved the country life and we sometimes visited gamekeepers who I suppose he knew through supplies. I never met any of his family connections other than Aunt Annie in Leeds who was married to a shoe shop owner in Roundhay called Sam Webster.

We visited the Websters sometimes for a day and I later went by train to stay for a week, as their daughter Alma was my age.

I had few relations and no grandparents. My mother had an old father, I only saw once on a day visit to Newland Park. I was told in later years he had been in a home in Hull as an alcoholic! A few aunts and an uncle occasionally visited from Birmingham. The Andrews kept in touch with mother and her girls, but her husband was never heard of after going to Australia, so I expect she could re-marry through desertion. I imagine the girls (my half sisters) were not so pleased to have their surnames changed to Oxtoby. Everything in those days hinged on respectability!

I didn't even know mother had been married before until I was about twelve, and asked why the name Andrews was used on old postcards kept in an album I was looking through. I got a very brief answer!

Olive left the convent at sixteen and had some 'book-keeping' training before going into Father's office. She always had lots of boyfriends around and a few lively girl friends too.

Lallie didn't 'work' in my memory. I once heard she'd had a "nervous breakdown". Lill didn't have a very good opinion of Lallie, somehow classing her as having "big ideas"!

She certainly had smart clothes and gave a dance once when the dancing to a gramophone took place in the long hall. I remember an orange dress of chenille velvet low cut with narrow shoulder straps in what was known as "flapper" style. It had a fringed stoke to match and many years later I had it dyed black and used it when I went to dances!

Lallie, rather hastily, at twenty five gave up a current and rather pleasant boyfriend Don Penrose, to marry Eric Pearce who had recently returned from the Argentine. He was dashing, glamorous, and swept Lallie 'off her feet'! His father a land-agent lived opposite us in Newland Park with a tiny wife. Their daughter Peggy died at a young age. The wedding was arranged with speed as Eric planned to sail for Canada (like an unknown country to us) where he had plans to make a fortune! He had been a first world war R.A.F. pilot and was a trained engineer, we were told, and in his youth attracted to the stage and acted with Mrs Patrick Campbell, an early Edwardian actress of some fame!

I remember some of the lovely "trousseau" my mother supplied (who paid Lallie's dress allowance all those years if she didn't have a job?) There was a brocade coat with fur collar, and a fur coat as well as numerous dresses, hats, bags and gloves 'all to match" in those days.

A huge cabin trunk was bought. I was intrigued by this as it opened out with hanging space on one side and a set of drawers on the other.

The wedding, as many were in that period, was simple. Lallie wore a longish blue dress with matching hat. Olive and I were ill matched bridesmaids – there are no photographs, in fact, I don't even remember any! - so different from to-day's 'must' of a few hundred pounds worth.

I have what was known as a 'studio portrait' of mother in her bride's mum outfit. A beautiful black dress with an over-shirt – long sleeves and elegant pleated blouse effect in pale pink. The waistline was low in the fashion of the day.

Little Irene was dressed in a white frilly affair with straw hat. My shoes were white too – "buckskin" said mother as we tried them on in Dolcis shop. I didn't like outfits like that and seldom wore them. I also never wore again the frilly lace knickers.

The 'Reception' must have been low-key, and at the bungalow, and after that a honeymoon in Sandsend before Lallie and Eric sailed off to Canada. Their life was vastly different to anything anticipated by all parties concerned.

Eric's high hopes of making a fortune were soon dashed! They lived in a shack high in the Rockies trying vainly to find gold - yes literally! Lallie, so undomesticated, had to learn to keep house in the most primitive conditions, to wear dungarees, while post was flung on an embankment from passing trains!

In old age, Lallie wrote of this experience, and the copy could be added to my story. Later they survived in Vancouver for a few years before returning home destitute with two year old Harvey. The families having cabled the fare for return voyage!

Before leaving the Newland Park period, I must mention dogs, as I have always been a doggy person.

First there was Chunky an oversized Yorkshire terrier – very hairy, and a character I loved to play with. Sadly on an afternoon visit to Bridlington he disappeared forever! Mother and Lill went to the shops, my friend Pam and I went for a walk on the beach – and each thought Chunky was with the other. We called and called his name, informed the police and advertised, but poor Chunky must have been picked up by someone – hopefully to be loved. Pam and I were very subdued on the return journey.

I have photos of Betsey the Airedale. She had eleven puppies and was famous in the family for having reared ten, while one of the cats reared the smallest having recently been deprived of drowned kittens as was the custom! We kept one puppy from the litter called Rough and he lived until I was in my late teens, a very dear dog.

I must also record a little about food and meals at Newland Park. Breakfast cereals as today were not known, but Force was popular and I loved it. I have an idea Mother liked Grape-Nuts, but Force had a colourful packet with "Sunny Jim" pictured on one side. You could save tokens and send for a stuffed model. The verse which accompanied this figure ran "over the fence jumps Sunny Jim, Force is the food that raises him!" I was a faddy eater in some ways and recall having a plate of Force for Christmas Dinner! I never cared for "greens" which Lill served always with the hot midday meal.

She made wonderful puddings and I loved them all. Steamed varieties were popular in all forms. Pies – never crumbles – were good too – plenty of fruit in season.

Fresh meat from the butcher, delivered, as was the fish, was frequently on the table; Dover sole, halibut with shrimp sauce, crabs and lobsters. Fish pies and "potted fish" which was made from leftover halibut and eaten like pate today. Milk puddings of all kinds including a strange one called 'apple and tappi' - a recipe from a Norwegian neighbour in Dover Street days.

Teas on Thursdays (Father's half day) were always a fish dish. We always used fish knives and forks and had large serviettes for silver rings. Also a silver-plated container in which to stand a tomato sauce bottle! Thinly cut bread and butter always for tea.

Best china was in constant use. I have the remnants of the blue, red and gold rather like a Crown Derby pattern, tureens, sauceboats with china stands and matching ladles. Silver, which needed frequent polishing, and got it, always appeared for tea and dinner. We never had "lunch" or "supper" or evening dinner parties. Perhaps we were in the "lower middle class" bracket!

Even in summer, gloves were worn in the street – one never ate in the street either and all adults wore hats and school children too.

Everyone smoked! Even mother and Lill joined the long cigarette holder brigade with "cork-tips" – Craven A or De–Resk, which had the best cards for my collection. Square cards with watercolour scenes of the countryside were favourites.

We had "Gin & It" in the house for a time, but not after Christian Science took over. Only my sisters and friends had cigarettes and "drinks"! Father had beer and the odd cigar.

Lemonade came in the bottles with marbles in the top. I still have a wooden gadget necessary to dislodge the marble.

Lill made lovely ice cream in a wooden tub-like machine. There was a central metal container surrounded with packed ice (which could be delivered with the fish) and one vigorously turned a handle till the mixture of milk, cream, vanilla essence and eggs turned into yellow ice cream! It had to be eaten quite quickly as there were no fridges.

Christmas was over quickly, compared with the new century, just two days really, and post came on December 25th but not on Boxing Day. We had a real tree, of course, and I still have two little ornaments from that time. Real candles were clipped on the branches. We all had "stockings" on Christmas Eve and I had a pillowcase well filled. Once I thought I'd been too naughty when I woke early to see a limp linen case hanging on the iron bed rail! It proved to be my nightdress case (why were such things a "must"?) so I soon found a bulging pillowcase propped up at the bed end. Always a huge turkey – lots of stuffing – Palethorpes sausages, potatoes and other vegetables. How did Lill manage it all? No heated trolley, and old type gas cooker, but I think an old range would keep things hot. The pudding was brought in ablaze and a good rum sauce. We had crackers, of course, but not much decoration other than holly behind the pictures and bunches of mistletoe.

The large dish for a turkey or large joint was often used and is still in good condition, Sylvan scenes in sepia tint and a deep well for the gravy to settle.

Strangely Mother always carved. Father sat back at ease. A diamond in his tiepin and heavy watch chain with seal and a little sovereign case dangling from it and his watch carefully tucked in a waistcoat pocket. While eating, all this was carefully obscured by the white table napkin, (we called them serviettes in the common fashion!) which was tucked in his shirt collar.

Christmas day was one of the few times my parents played a board game or cards with me. I read at an early age and loved my books. If I had a Christmas time party as many friends did, Lallie would help to entertain and was very good at it. Once she and friend Don organised a game where each child was blindfold in turn in the hall and led into the room where an aeroplane waited! I remember still being helped to stand on what was a plank between two stools and with arms round the necks of the helpers being lifted 'high in the air' with appropriate swinging and engine noises before a careful "landing". Funnily enough I never tried this game on my children! I can however recall the excitement.

Lill excelled at party teas, and apart from jelly we always had a dish of drained tinned peach halves filled with whipped cream and cherries and 'handles' of strips of angelica! Late in life my old friends remembered

Lill's wonderful egg sandwiches.

So ended life at Oimara, 32 Newland Park. I knew nothing of the reasons for the sale, or the adverts or showing people round, or even what type of people bought it. I'm sure a nine year old would know all about everything today

I do know the family thought it would be a great blow to me, but with a fairly calm nature, and perhaps a gift for accepting change, I was pleased to be going to 112 Park Avenue, near my friends from school, Pam, Betty and Jill. I'm told Lill wept as she locked the bungalow door. I expect it was a "come-down" for my parents and Mother might have missed her poultry and the veranda and garden. They didn't lead a social life. The Alisons, next door, never came calling or for a meal. Neither did the Fords opposite in spite of my friendship with little Jack.

Lallie had friends, the Crosslands who lived in a large house on the corner of Cottingham Road, as their daughter Dorothy (she had three 'Dorothy' friends) played bridge and tennis.

Olive's friends did not live near, and my friend Joan Newell with whom I started my interest in dancing classes at Tommy Fosters was at Newland High School. We lost touch till later in life when she came to the Hull Theatre as an actress. At my early parties she was a star performer when anyone willing would get up and recite. I loved doing my turns, but Joan even then was a natural and got much applause.

Once we had a gigantic Christmas cracker to pull, and the little guests scrambled for the presents as they scattered over the carpet. Mother said afterwards the grown-ups were amused by a little Jewish boy Aubrey Zudoffsky calling "who will have this one for tuppence?"

Irene and mother outside the bungalow, Newland Park

Four year old Irene with parents & half-sister Lallie

Irene with beloved bear Peter, Newland Park garden

Irene 9 months

Fred Oxtoby in chicken run, Newland Park

Irene dancing - Cave Castle Garden Party

Jacky Ford and Irene - dressing up in Fords garden

Tommy Foster Dancers at Hull City Hall. Early Thirties. Irene in middle

Irene, Mickey & Joan - Convent Pupils

Irene & Pam on top of Scafell

Lill with Rough and Bon, Park Avenue

Alice Oxtoby, Newland Park

112 PARK AVENUE

The Park Avenue house was one of four in a terrace with passages between two, giving access to the back door (for tradesmen!) and garden. The passage had two doors at the end, set at an angle, but I seldom bumped into anyone from 110 with dogs or bike. As in Newland Park we hardly knew any neighbours.

The four houses were built of pale brick, almost yellow and had high gables over bay windows at the front for the main bedroom and another bay for the dining room. A tiny front garden with a small lawn where mother had a red umbrella shaped rambler rose tree planted in the centre. It was trained over a wire cage and flowered well in the summer.

At the back, the garden consisted of a long lawn, flowerbeds, and a sycamore tree and vegetable patch. All quite private with no over looking to 'next doors'.

Father had been anxious to give me swings and rings, built in substantial wooden frames. The rings went rough when weather affected them and I longed for smooth leather bound type, which my friend Maureen had in her 'nursery' upstairs in Westbourne Avenue.

Beyond the swings was a large garage complete with pit let into the floor. Mother once sprained her ankle badly when it was left uncovered after the car had been serviced.

We still kept a few hens and they lived in a wired off enclosure near the door into a back entry for vehicles, a feature of all the avenues, originally for horse drawn vehicles.

Decorators had been busy before we moved in and the whole house done up in the latest style. This consisted of elaborate wallpaper designs with panels of birds, flowers or abstract motifs surrounded by borders with plain paper "surrounds". It sounds ghastly and it probably was!

There were five bedrooms and again one bathroom and separate loo.

I had a back room with bay window over looking the garden. The family before us had used this room as a nursery and installed a small lift in which meals (and perhaps laundry) could be pulled up and down from the scullery!

My friends and I thought this was fun and Lill would put in sandwiches, buns etc for our teas which could be eaten at a small set of white painted wooden chairs and table which stood in the window. I was sorry later in life that this table and chairs which had been in the family a long time, were passed on to sister Olive's family and I never saw them again!

My close friend Pam Owen lived at No.13 Park Avenue and we always walked to school together. I never used my bike on school days in the Avenues, as Pam didn't ride one.

Pam's father, a sea captain, had died when she was very young and her Mother was plump, pleasant and well educated. Not as energetic as my Mother and I seem to visualise her mostly lounging on the old green velvet sofa. Pam's older sisters Theo and Mon helped with housekeeping, though sometimes there was a maid in the kitchen. Theo was a 'dispenser' for a local Doctor and Mon was a matron at her Uncle's boarding school in Windermere.

Pam and I played a lot of card or board games in what was the 'nursery' overlooking the garden. It was also the dining room as the more grand and formal dining room at the front was seldom used. In there stood a heavy, ornately carved sideboard – probably mahogany and brought from India by Pam's father. We were fascinated by large carved figures of "foreign" men. Three I think, and one was loose in his niche, and could be gently pulled out, to be carefully examined. This sideboard is still in the Owen family and much admired.

Sometimes we had the excitement of 'staying the night' in each other's houses with midnight feasts laid on as we both read avidly the schoolgirl annuals, and storybooks – mostly about secret goings-on in the 'dorm'.

Funnily enough 'pomegranates' were often part of our feast – messy for bedclothes I would think!

On the nursery wall there was an engraving of the "Last Supper". Pam's grandfather had been Vicar of St. Augustine's in Hull, one of his daughters had turned Catholic and become a Nun – Mother Cecilia – at the French Convent and taught us art. It was rather strange that Pam's sister joined the Catholic Church and Pam in middle age also followed this family trend.

In Bugthorpe Church to-day there is what seems like the same picture of the last supper, and seeing it, takes me back to the nursery of Pam's house in Park Avenue, which also had a large, and well loved rocking horse in the bay window.

We were both "tomboys" with a love of climbing trees in our back gardens. I once fell out of a sycamore in our garden, and chipped a piece off a centre bottom jaw tooth. No fuss was made of such falls and I rarely visited a dentist and the chipped tooth stayed till I inevitably acquired dentures!

Another tomboy game was re-arranging furniture in Pam's nursery, or my kitchen so we could indulge in a climbing activity of "going round the room without touching the floor". Our kitchen was quite a large square room with a table big enough for breakfast, for baking on, homework for me, or for use in dressmaking sessions. Mother was expert on the Singer treadle machine, and Lill did cutting out, hand sewing and "finishing off" jobs. I had dozens of cotton frocks in summer – all with "knickers to match". They were made in simple styles – mostly sleeveless and bias binding much in evidence. Sometimes they were contrived from the best parts of Mother's worn out dresses. I loved the feel and colours of Macclesfield silk, which she favoured – mostly in stripes. Later I had "Liberty" materials, sent for from catalogues, or the popular 'Tobacco' with pretty patterns of summer flowers.

Our dining room was at the front of the house and still large enough for the big sideboard and plush covered settee (Chesterfield) and chairs as well as mahogany extending table with high backed chairs.

The drawing room with French window on to the yard, and garden beyond was used constantly and had a coal fire. In the kitchen we had a big black "Cook and Heat" stove, which also heated radiators throughout the house.

There was also a scullery and pantry and gas stove for cooking too. An electric boiler for washday and up to date "Acme" wringer with rubber rollers.

While in Park Avenue I can't leave out dogs again! Rough the Airedale was still with us and lived to a good age, but soon after moving from Newland Park I was given a wonderful present – a Pekinese puppy! I know many dog lovers can't stand Pekes, but "Bon", short for "Bonzo" a popular doggie name at that time was so sweet in spite of big eyes and squashed nose!

Mrs Crosland, a relation of Lallie's friend had told Mother of her litter of pups, so off we went, with Lill to Ferriby to see them. I remember the day well, also the big garden where we were taken to see an unusual sight – a cuckoo taking up all available space in a small nest almost hidden in a tall hedge. I have never seen one since!

Bon was brought out, admired and bought. I was given instructions on how to care for this bundle of fur, and told I should have a wicker kennel for the house as he would need rest and peace sometimes, and a good bed for night time. So a small indoor kennel was bought and proved very satisfactory with the little dog peering out of the slatted door or sleeping soundly on layers of newspaper.

Bon grew to be a great friend, and very lively, and I even dressed him in doll's clothes to push out in my beautiful big pram, which I rarely played with. Later in life that same pram came back for my little girls, having been lent out for years.

Rough and Bon caused amusement when being exercised in the avenues as such a contrast. They were well behaved too. We didn't have tinned food for them, but I would be sent to a local butcher's shop for "Two pound of fowpenny pieces please".

All meat and fish had to be bought frequently as there were no fridges or freezers.

Lill loved both dogs and wept when they died at a good age, after I left home for good.

My friend Betty, known as Bunky left Marlborough Avenue as her family moved "down south" to Braintree. However we kept in touch by letters and in the holidays visited each other, which was great fun.

I remember being "put on" the London train to be met by Betty and her father at Kings Cross. Mr Barrow was very good about showing me London, and on one occasion we went up the Monument near Billingsgate. I was in my teens then. Braintree was wonderful! A house with an apple orchard (commercial project) and a tennis court. Bunky was at a rare 'co-ed' grammar school, so boys were our friends too, with lots of tennis parties, cycle rides, and of all things a "sun lido" open air swimming pool on the outskirts of the town.

I was lucky in having holidays to remember with joy to this day, with Pam and her family, as they were glad of a friend of Pam's age, and my parents didn't seem able to get away.

One year when we were eleven we had three glorious weeks in Devon! Mrs Owen, Theo, Pam and I boarding in a thatched cottage on the one street – a winding steep lane to the tiny harbour of Buck's Mills.

The train journey had been exciting, but the cottage life was wonderful. All cooking done for us and nice rooms, but no "mod cons". We washed in bedroom bowls on "washstands" – used po's and went down the garden path where the little privy was built over the stream which wound its way to the sea with other such little sheds similarly sited! I must say it was draughty at times! The sun shone daily, and we bathed, had picnic lunches on the rocks while avoiding the part of the beach where the stream cascaded down the steep cliffs!

Along the cliffs we could see the white string of buildings, which was Clovelly, and opposite was magic (to me) the Island of Lundy. I had to wait until I was seventy to visit it and still found it magical.

Socks were never worn in summer and if we were chilly we had school blazers to wear over dresses. We needed all those cotton frocks and knickers as no washing was done for us! In the evenings Pam and I enjoyed reading 'Chums' annuals, which had belonged to our landlady's son Stuart who was now an R.A.F. pilot, and was known to have flown over his parent's home! Like most of the villagers the surname was Braund.

Mrs Owen was interested to know that the Churchill family owned a holiday house near the harbour, explaining to us that Winston Churchill was Chancellor of the Exchequer, which meant little to us! His daughter Sarah who later became an actress was often on the beach as was the toddler Mary who was with her Nanny. I even remember a knitted 'beach-suit' she wore – in brown wool – Mary not the Nanny!

When we joined a village group for a 'paper-chase' on the cliffs one afternoon Sarah was there in a frock of trobaloc with buttercup pattern like one of mine! She later married Vic Oliver who died young. Mary then became Lady Soames and wrote a biography of Lady Churchill.

We did leave Bucks Mills some times, and visited by bus Bideford, Hartland Point and Clovelly. We returned to Yorkshire very suntanned.

I must include Jill Evans in my list of local school friends, though I never had the 'kindred spirit' feeling as with Pam and Betty. Adrienne who lived in Salisbury Street adjoining the avenues went away to school at Ascot and I have often written of her and her sister's lovely matching dresses, and the fact that she was co-author with me in writing a play when I was 12 and she 11 in my book "Overalls and sashes".

I am trying to avoid repetition of earlier books so will miss out convent details.

Dr Evans lived in a big double fronted house on Princes Avenue; Mrs Evans was of German descent and a charming lady, always very kind to me, as was the Doctor. There were two older brothers; we didn't see a lot of them. Peter was at university in Birmingham and Mark who would go into the firm "Premier Oil and Soap Company" spent some time after Hymers' College in Germany. He became keen on the 'Blackshirts' and Hitler's influence and got Mrs Evans to make a black sweater with swastika motif!

Jill was lonely in some ways and used to often phone me to say, "are you coming round?" or "can you stay the night?"

They had a housemaid and a cook who stayed in the kitchen. I remember us laughing at thumps and bumps sounding out to the hall as Dorothy and Mary practised handstands against the door! Jill and I had a craze for handstands against the landing doors – with shoes off first, of course!

The dining room there became a waiting room for "panel patients" (free I suppose) who sat on dining chairs lined up against the walls after breakfast was cleared, or before the evening meal. The surgery was next door, and an everyday sitting room across the hall. Upstairs there was a smart drawing room for entertaining. Jill and I used single beds in the guest room, which was bare and sparse. Linoleum and rugs on the floor, and a gas fire in winter was nice for dressing.

Jill had a tiny bedroom over the front door and the boys had a big attic room. There was also a billiard room up there, formerly a nursery. With all these members of the household there was one loo with washbasin on the halfway landing and one bathroom! No loo in there. I think there must have been one for the maids "out at the back". We rarely went to the kitchens.

I learnt quite a lot of social behaviour as the Evans sometimes gave dinner parties to which Jill and I were permitted to join before the adults went upstairs for bridge. I learnt to eat different courses and saw such unfamiliar things as a whole Stilton, onto which Dr. Evans poured port, or having croutons for soup.

I often felt a little uncomfortable on such occasions, especially after Jill said one night "I don't know what they'll think of you Oxo!" A tradesman's daughter in a professional gathering! I must have been rather an oddity!

It is strange now to think that as young teenagers Jill and I shared a morning bath, during which Dr. Evans would rush in wearing blue matching undergarments to use the washbasin saying, "Don't mind me Occy" his name for me rather than "Oxo". There was more class distinction then and I remember Jill once saying that her mother decided there were only a few real 'ladies' in school and one was Mickey! Some times Dr. Evans decided to take us for an afternoon drive. They had their favourite places not far away. I remember Wauldby Green near Brantingham Dale, Londesborough Park. and Wansford near the river.

The Doctor and Mrs Evans would sit out on rugs, or chairs reading, or walk with Jill and me. Tea from flasks and a piece of cake as there was a substantial 'supper' on return.

Jill and I loved card games on evenings together or just reading. She was a plain girl, very neat with narrow plaits and rather smart clothes.

Before leaving the Evans family I must record the sad fact that Jill took her own life when aged about 40. She became a dietician and had mental illnesses. I visited Dr and Mrs Evans briefly after the war, when they lived in the kitchen, no maids, and were still very kind to me. They spoke little of Jill who even then was having difficulties coping with life. She had longed for a romantic, social success, which seemed to pass her by. A wasted life indeed! I still use the stoneware jug she gave me for my 21st and the dinner service from the Evans family is at Cot Nab.

During the 112 Park Avenue years, my sister Olive married Dale Briggs, who had a laundry in the town, in a quiet ceremony at St Augustine's Church and I with her friend Nora were bridesmaids. I think I was 14, and looked dreadful in a long green crepe dress with wide green organdie frills on the elbow length sleeves. It was never worn again!

The family had been devastated, and disorganised by the return in poverty of Eric and Lallie with two-year-old son Harvey from Canada. A shock to hear they had run out of money and jobs, and their parents had to finance the voyage home.

All this family trauma happened before Olive married, so she still needed her bedroom. I was the one expected to give up my room overlooking the garden, with three quarter size bed, which I'd shared with visiting friends. To make it better for me, Mother had the bedroom over the front door decorated. I could choose the curtains, and the new furniture that was mass produced, dressing table, wardrobe and two drawer chest in what mother called "plywood". I liked it, and also chose a tall, narrow, glass fronted bookcase with "leaded" effect on the glass and oval top. A little bedside oak table completed this set and I was quite happy. My "Margaret Tarrant" pictures went on the walls and collection of little ornaments on the top of the drawers; I felt comfortable and was never one to be upset by change.

It was not easy for Lallie, Eric and Harvey to be added to the household, and disturbing for them after the high hopes of life in Canada. The smart honeymoon clothes were shabby, and it was left to my parents and senior Pearces to help to clothe them.

Eric got a succession of mediocre jobs and I'm vague how long this situation lasted. Eric was a cinema commissionaire and then he started Pearce's Parcel Delivery Service for shops and firms wishing to send parcels to suburbs or outlying residential villages. Naturally he had a smartly tailored uniform made to match his brown and gold motorbike and sidecar type of vehicle. I later realised Lill had found life difficult while they were with us. This did not make out well, so off he went to Brazil – and after securing a job in Rio-de-Janeiro, he sent money for Lallie and Harvey to follow! For a time all went well with Eric teaching in an English school and Lallie taught English to the Ambassador's daughter. I was interested in Lallie's letters from Rio, and the snaps of Harvey under a banana tree or Lallie and Eric under palms by a swimming pool. Lallie's pupil Isabelita , Lady Guerney's daughter sounded to have a luxurious lifestyle and Lallie was driven to and from the Embassy by car. Later in life, her references from Lady Guerney helped her to get into teaching jobs.

In Park Avenue life continued with my Father becoming ill, and Mother taking over some of the office management.

I was less involved with the dancing classes at Tommy Fosters, though I had loved them also taking part in displays in special dresses, and did more elocution exams with a private teacher Constance Clark. I loved taking part in anything to do with drama at school and started going to the Repertory Theatre sometimes with Mother and Lill. Going to the pictures had been a must most Saturdays. Being a teenager didn't mean a sudden 'growing up' stage as it does today, but having periods was a nuisance and at first Mother provided home-made protection! No warning that one might start menstruation either! It was known in our household with Lill's name for it "being queer"!!

I suppose the old ways of making squares of worn out linen sheets, or table linen were the normal habits, as some people took a long time to adjust and pay for disposable towels as with babies' nappies in this day and age. But I can't imagine why Mother and Lill chose to soak the things and wash and iron them too! I had 'bought' ones for holidays, which was a relief. I had two memorable holidays with the Owens in the Lake District, staying with them in the Grammar School in Windermere. No boys there, of course, Pam's Uncle was Headmaster and on holiday himself. It was an ideal holiday place for Pam and me; we had beds in a dormitory and a bath each in the ablutions section. We revelled in using the gym whenever we liked, and put on a 'display' for the grown ups one evening. I remember we called ourselves the Red 'O's' being Owen and Oxtoby, and also both had by chance dresses made up in the same patterned red cotton (knickers to match as always) we could wear them for our display.

My Mother had a rare holiday with us for a few days during that fortnight and drove us around. We had Mon with us for mountain climbing as being a matron to her headmaster Uncle she was used to expeditions with the schoolboys.

Pam and I did stiff climbs – even Scafell Pike – wearing our school shoes with socks. Pam did have a pair of flannel shorts, but I was considered too fat for such garments and cheerfully climbed in a cotton frock carrying a Mac in case of rain!

We also swam in the lake, and played tennis on the school courts. While exploring the playing field we found urinals in the pavilion and were quite surprised!

Another year we had a rented cottage near Ambleside, and another exciting holiday. I still love visits to the Lakes and can remember the names of mountains taught to us by Mon.

Mrs Owen had Theo for company when we were climbing. We all got around on buses and seldom ate out. Pam and I loved the pencil shop in Keswick and bought some with our names on and some to take back for friends. We also loved a shop in Windermere where you could buy miniature bronze figures, hand painted of Beatrix Potter figures for 2/6! I still have Pigling Bland.

During the summer when I was fourteen we met the Megginsons! The family had discovered the quiet beach at Fraisthorpe. Actually Auburn Sands where a village had been washed away by the sea! One farm remained and half an old cottage actually on the low cliff or sand dunes and there was plenty of parking space. Here a farmer's wife, Mrs Smith, sold pots of tea to picnicking visitors and we were frequent visitors at weekends. It is quite true that many pre-war summers were really hot and sunny! My parents, Lill and Ethel donned swimming costumes, though I don't think any could actually swim! They bought a striped tent for shelter from winds, and in which we could all get changed. Sometimes Olive and Dale joined us and I have a group 'snap' with Eric, Lallie, Harvey with their friends too. I often took friends, but on that occasion Alma from Leeds was visiting us.

My father was not well, the beginning of a long illness, cancer of the pancreas I believe, but 'cancer' was a word seldom heard. The bathing suited him and they decided to ask at a farmhouse in the village, if it was possible to stay overnight on Saturdays to save the drive back to Hull.

I wasn't with them the night they called at Manor House, but Mr Megginson showed them round as his wife had been driven to see relations on the Wolds. He told them they had recently moved from a Wold farm and they hoped to take summer visitors!

The next week I went too and all was arranged for Father, Mother, Lill and me to stay Saturday night. The first of many visitors for Nellie Megginson to look after. I thought it all quite wonderful! I loved the farm, the animals, especially the carthorses and a hunter called Darkie. The farmer's son Jack was 21, but we were soon friends. His sister, Christine, was a year younger than me, but a nice girl and I liked her too. Another sister Dorothy lived at home.

I was so taken up with the farm, I asked if I could stay for all the summer holiday! Mrs Megginson said, "Yes if I lived as family" because she would be booked up some of the time with other visitors. That suited me fine. I admit I didn't relish in not having a bathroom and the three hole little houses down the garden path were not a joy to visit. The oil lamps and the candles were a nuisance too and pos were under the bed, which I shared with Chris. Because of 'visitors' we slept at the back of the house in Jack's bedroom and Jack had a bed in a hut in the paddock that was a new henhouse, but bought to make a bedroom. A mattress was laid on wooden supports nailed to the walls!

Meals for 'family' were eaten in the big farmhouse kitchen, which had a vast coal, fired range with hot water 'boiler' at one side. There was also an even bigger 'wall' oven with its own fire underneath. This was used for big baking days.

There were two tables, one for meals or 'sitting round' and the other for baking, food preparation or for washing up in a deep zinc bowl with tin tray for draining the pots.

The sink – a flat stone one was in the back kitchen and had a pump on either side, one drinking water and the other 'soft' from the well. Dairy utensils were washed here and pans. The two farm lads had a table in a small room next to the 'copper house' used on washday, so their meals were carried through. They slept in the 'men's room' up the back staircase.

Meals were different from home with more pastry and home made bread. I liked bread and butter, toast and all the pies and puddings. Meat was alright, but not the fat, so I never had the bacon. I wasn't keen on green vegetables at that time.

Chris and I helped to lay tables and to wash up. Dorothy and her mother were always working - Edward must have been a good baby – and the men needed lots of baking for the 'lowances' as well as big meals. With visitors in the dining room with far more 'posh' food, I don't know how they managed, even with Mrs Wilson in the village coming in to help out. Of course, one didn't have to go shopping in 'Brid' very often as trade vans called regularly, not only the butcher and grocer, but chemist and drapers.

I've written about Manor House and the time there with Jack in my 'Mud' books, and in "A life on the Wolds" but in this epistle I am trying to include little extras to show life's changes.

The grocery van came to Fraisthorpe every two weeks preceded by Mr Knott from Mennells in Bridlington who came by car. He took the order sitting at the kitchen table, and when there was a pause he'd prompt Jack's mother with such remarks as "any suet this time Mrs 'Er". We all took off his "Mrs 'Er" part. I suppose it saved giving his customers their names.

The orders were large, with flour bought by the stone and tipped into a wooden bin, which stood on the brick floor of the dairy. It had a hinged lid and one used a scoop to get flour out in quantities estimated for the day's baking. Weighing was done with the old heavy scales with little metal weights. Not so little if making up seven pounds for bread. I think 2lbs was the heaviest for those scales, but a 'scoop' would be hand made by a blacksmith and hold one pound at least.

I remember hearing that the draper chap was rather inclined to personal remarks, such as looking up to the airing rack where the week's laundry would be hanging and saying "Well Missus! If them's the best bloomers, its time you had some new 'uns!'".

Groceries when delivered were unpacked on the dairy shelf. The meat, which came twice weekly, had to be stored in the coolest place, (dairies always faced north) and be protected from flies in summer, as there was nothing in the way of refrigeration.

I remember Chris and I sharing a bath in a tin utensil filled with water from the range. The bath was put on the brick tiled kitchen floor and doors locked and curtains drawn for privacy!

The bucket-closet down the garden path with a single compartment, plus a double seater next door was one of the drawbacks of country living, as also the use of bedroom chamber pots. In spite of all this the summer holidays at "the farm" were an absolute joy to me.

I was not really aware that my Father's illness was terminal. I remember he sat in a sitting room chair a lot, but he was always a rather remote figure to me, as growing older we had few common interests.

Eventually he was confined to bed with Lill and Ethel doing most of the nursing, and Mother busy looking after the shop.

I remember little of his death, only telling Pam on the phone that he had died, and I would miss school for a day or two. I didn't go to the funeral as younger people, especially females were not expected to. I know he was cremated as my Mother had once expressed her horror in burying her much loved daughter Ethel on a pouring wet day. Graves were not important to Mother and I never remember her visiting any. I have the same feelings about "earthly remains".

WE MOVE TO THE LESS FASHIONABLE
END OF THE AVENUE.

We were in a poor way financially after Father's death. The car was sold and eventually the house also sold, and we moved to a smaller, three bedroom house at the far end of Park Avenue No. 139. There was a pleasant garden at the back and I still had the dogs, Rough and Bon. Lill and I were left together quite a lot. I saw Mickey frequently and out of school we would meet in town to catch glimpses of the repertory actors, who were so important to us as 'stage struck' teenagers.

I was not pressurised to take exams at school as children are now. I managed to pass "Junior Oxford" but as maths was a must for "Senior" which followed, there was no hope for me!

I think Mother got fees reduced in my last year. I took extra painting classes and elocution, passing exams for "Elo" with distinction. Out of school I loved the cinema and the Repertory theatre plays.

After leaving the convent at 16, I sometimes wonder how I filled in the days! I would browse in second hand bookshops, listen to the radio and sometimes went to the roller-skating rink on Anlaby Road. A boy called Percy was often there and I enjoyed the "dancing" to all those popular tunes. "These foolish things", "Too much in love to say goodnight", "Be sure its true when you say I love you, it's a sin to tell a lie" and the jokey ones like "It ain't no sense sitting on a fence – all by yourself in the moonlight". I remember all those silly verses even now.

That Christmas I managed to get in the chorus (dancing) for the Repertory Theatre

Production of "Alice in Wonderland" and had three weeks of bliss! So many of the cast went on to the West End, or films, and James Stewart changed his name to Stewart Grainger to become a film star. Some have lingered on to be in T.V. over the years.

I played tennis at the courts on Cottingham Road, meeting up with Pam who was at the Art School doing architecture. She had a few boy friends there that joined us. One student John Woolley became quite a serious friend of mine, but he was so correct, and nothing physical in the relationship. We read the same books and went to the odd dance. He could drive his father's car (they lived in Newland Park) but didn't take it out in rain! He was very much the only child and devoted son.

Mickey had left Cottingham and was living in London with her Mother and became a student at the R.A.D.A. I would have loved that, but it was not financially possible. Joan in spite of a good matriculation result decided to take up a career with horses.

In 2005 while watching tennis at Queen's Club, my thoughts went back to pre-war visits to Queen's Club Gardens where Mickey and her dear mother Edith de Coundouroff lived. They had a pleasant flat in the old style, which one catches a glimpse of on T.V. I'd guess there were about a hundred similar flats around the gardens in the middle where residents had a key.

Mickey was at the R.A.D.A. at this time, but we must have arranged visits in holiday times, and I remember stopping off on my way to Devon. I have such exciting memories, as Edith-de-C was good about arranging visits to theatres, and one to the Theatrical Garden Party held I think that year at Hurlingham. I met Noel Coward; at least he borrowed my 'posh' propelling pencil to sign a programme for me. We saw dozens of theatricals (not known then as 'celebs') and I loved every minute of it.

The visits to theatres to see such plays as Dodie Smith's "Call it a Day" and other what were known as "drawing room comedies" and J B Priestley types. We queued for the 'pit' and paid for stools in the waiting time. There were some entertainers to while away the waits, and I remember one man who did extraordinary contortions to turn his clothes inside out! Seats there cost one shilling and six pence.

We also went shopping, Mickey and I, to the Kensington stores quite near – "Derry and Toms", "Pontings" and another "Barkers". I bought an 'edge to edge' coat in brown – high fashion and one wore a coat when dressed up even on hot days. Thin material and lace gloves to match, I still have those!

A favourite dress was a bright multi-patterned one. Gathered bodice with 2 short diagonal zips in black, slanting from the neck! Zips were quite new and with puff sleeves, a belt and full skirt this became a favourite of Jacks later.

These clothes would be considered unbelievably cheap compared even with changes in money values today. £2 was extravagant, and in Selfridges Bargain Basement I found a rayon all over patterned dress – zigzag oriental – with an elastic waist and known as dirndl style. It cost three shillings and six pence and I wore it for years after my marriage and the waist expansion was useful when pregnant!

I forgot to say Mickey bought a similar "edge-to-edge" coat in black when I got the brown – mine had a loose belt of the same material from side seams, but Mikey's caught up at the waist with a loop and button. We thought we looked elegant with light summer dresses showing down the front.

I loved the modern furnishings in the London flat with a lovely divan in the sitting room, covered in pale green, and cushions in green and pale lemon piled on top. I had a bedroom, but Mickey or her mother must have slept on the divan when having a guest.

Neither Mickey nor I were brought up to cook or to do housework and Edith de C. must have done it all. I remember a pudding (well, I would wouldn't I?) called "chocky mange" which Edith made – I expect we'd class it as a soufflé now. No fridge at that time – so frequent shopping for fresh supplies from what I think was Mile End Road, as we were really between Fulham and West Kensington.

When Mickey married after meeting Arthur as a warden in the air raids, they also had a flat in Queens Club Gardens, until moving to Norwich just after their fourth daughter was born.

I DECIDE TO TRAIN AS A GIRL GROOM

Aged fifteen Joan and I had both taken to riding at a small stable in Hornsea. Half a crown an hour and only a pair of cheap jodhpurs needed as equipment!

Joan heard of a riding school and guest house in Devon which took resident pupils and had been taken down for an interview. I think the cost was around £100 for six months, then a chance to work for one's keep and to get a job as a girl groom.

After Joan's letters, which were enthusiastic about this way of life, Mother decided she could afford to send me and it would be good for me to widen my outlook and to be less dependable on Lill!

I had to have a formidable list of clothes! Stable overalls, boots and leather leggings, as well as black hunting boots. Tweed jackets and a black one for hunting. Bowler and a felt hat for every day riding. Never jockey caps or head scarves. Also a Harry Hall riding mac, so quite an expensive set up.

I think someone gave me a travelling trunk (luggage in advance on the train) and I filled the bottom with my favourite books of plays and poetry!

I visited Mickey in London on the way down. Lovely to see West End plays and also spent two nights with Bunky (Betty Barrow) and her parents in Braintree.

It was a complete change of lifestyle to me to live in remote countryside on a small Devon farm, on the edge of Dartmoor. I've described this briefly in "Mud on my Doorstep" but it will seem unbelievable for any students of "equestrianism" today to hear of the way we lived!

Joan was becoming less happy there as Miss Haines, the bad tempered, owner of the 'establishment' could switch from mood to mood very quickly. She needed some girl to be available to vent her wrath on, and when a paid stable girl left, Joan became a victim. We were spoilt in a way, our boots were cleaned by the farm-hand, and our meals were cooked and served by "gentile" ladies, one an aunt of Miss Haines. We had no housework or washing jobs, but worked hard in the stables.

Good stable training, but our riding instruction was minimal in the 'visitor' time, we got little riding anyway as the house guests were all keen to ride. Our recreation was in talking to horses, mostly ponies as sure footed on the moor, when out in the fields on summer evenings or going for walks.

Church on Sunday mornings, writing letters (I kept up a lot of course) – reading, playing cards or monopoly which was brand new on dark evenings. No radio even, and lights out at 9 p.m. as electricity by generator, so reading in bed meant candles. We could have two baths per week!

Once a month we had a whole day off! We could go by a farmer's car for 2/6 to Newton Abbot to shop – eat in a café (lovely cream cakes) or even dash on a bus to Torquay! Such excitement!

Margery, a niece of Miss Haines, came down to work and that started a long lasting friendship as we got on extremely well. She was the daughter of a Wiltshire farmer and landowner and had her own horse.

The hunting days in winter bring back wonderful memories, and I loved the Devon countryside. It was quite a treat to be sent to get a pony shod in Widdecombe, in spite of the forge being surrounded by musical jugs and mugs with Widdecombe fair themes! When Joan found life too difficult under Miss Haines she left. There seemed less pupils and guests and after another six months working for keep I too left Dartmoor.

Margery left before I did and got jobs nearer home in Wiltshire. Being like me a compulsive letter writer, we corresponded every other week till her death before she was seventy quite suddenly when putting milk bottles on the step before going to bed.

I had been to stay in her family home in the village of Tidcombe when on holiday from Devon, and loved her mother, (father was more of a remote figure who managed the small estate) and got on well with her brother Paul. He was then at Radley, the public school at Abingdon, and I went with the family to 'Gaudy Day' there.

An experience I loved, not having been to a public school, though as a youngster I revelled in all the "Greyfriars" and "Magnet" boys' comics and annuals. We wore 'best' clothes for that day and Margery's Mum took a picnic. I was surprised to find she had packed gooseberry fool in a stone jar – it tasted delicious. Lill had never taken 'pudding' type food to a picnic. We watched cricket and went to Paul's study. While staying with Margery, we explored the old stables and I found a set of brass bells in a dusty cobwebby window. I was told no one wanted them, long since abandoned for carthorse decoration - and it took a lot of cleaning with vinegar and much rubbing with Brasso, before the brass surface was even visible.

Jack had a similar set which I was pleased to have in later years and today they are on a shelf in this cottage. I still polish them!

Also when on holiday, Joan drove me in their family car, having passed her test, and we visited the Megginsons after I'd seen in a local paper, that Jack had been winning gymkhana prizes! The Megginsons were pleased to welcome us, especially Jack, and he had a good pony called Flash. In the kitchen, a blue enamel Yorkist Range had replaced the big black leaded one, and mains water meant taps over the back kitchen sink and a bathroom upstairs! This, however, meant using a rotary pump before enough water for a bath could reach the bathroom! Twenty minutes of pushing a handle to and fro!

Jack, and his friend, and close neighbour, Henry Hyde shared a little Morris Coupe car, and at some stage they came to Hull Fair. Joan joined us and there was a panic in case Joan missed the Last train back to Hornsea as her father was very strict! Jack also came to the Fair with his friend Les Snowball and had tea at 112 Park Avenue first.

Jack's sister Dorothy had married Ted, and they lived at a farm at Habton, near Malton, having married when Edward was four.

I got a job with a family at Dartington, near Totnes. Mrs Champernowne was another strong character, but luckily I got on well with her, but it was her daughter Daphne France-Hayhurst I really worked with as she kept polo ponies for showing.

I never heard about Daphne's father, but her stepfather Tommy Champernowne had been part of the family who owned Dartington Hall which in recent years had been sold to the Elmhursts who ran it as an 'advanced' educational Hall with modern school, workshops, glass (to become a famous name) and of all things a nudist colony!

Mrs Champernowne strongly disapproved of all the Hall's activities – more so since her other daughter Betty had married an artist and writer called Toby Fitzwilliam who died young. I had enjoyed an amusing horsey book he'd written and illustrated which was in Miss Haines' bookcase.

Betty worked in London, and on her rare visits to 'Vineyard' seemed very sophisticated, but enjoyed a day's hunting.

'Vineyard' was a lovely old house standing alone, and high above the road to Plymouth from Totnes just before the village of Dartington. There were no indoor servants, just an ex-navy chap who did house cleaning and some of the cooking.

My living conditions to begin with were rather strange! There were two semi-detached workmen's cottages down a garden path and there was a communicating door downstairs. I had a pleasant little bedroom with a washstand complete with jug and washbowl – and a lavatory downstairs. My bed was damp, I'm sure as the first night I woke shivering with cold though it was autumn weather.

Next door to me, with sitting room, bedroom, bathroom and kitchen was Roland Fergusson! Aged forty, a bachelor, ex Indian Police Officer, tall, slim with thinning hair, but a pleasant manner and good sense of humour. He had retired from the Indian Police and was waiting to rent a cottage up on the moor, which belonged to the Champernownes, but was occupied.

Roland had many polo and pig –sticking trophies in his little sitting room and skins of lions and tigers on the floor! He called me each morning to have a mug of tea in his kitchen before I went to work and would wear an elegant Police cape over his pyjamas!

I found my stable work quite easy and grew fond of the ponies. The 'champion' was Thurl's Girl, commonly called Goose – a lovely bay mare. Roselight was grey and I was told with pride had 'Tetracht' spots on his coat. Good breeding I gather. Nigger, I forget his proper name, was almost black and had a habit of letting his tongue hang out to be stroked!

There was also an older pony, part Arab, called Azulada, Lulu for short and I was allowed to ride her.

Daphne was an expert rider (not the Miss Haine's style) and practised with a polo stick in readiness for showing. She was thirty at the time and we got on well together and often went into Totnes (to a milk bar!) or fly fishing where I stood by to watch even for 'sea trout' at night.

I had my meals at Vineyard and used the bathroom there. The front staircase was quite grand, with red carpet protected by white linen covers! We never used it, as the back stairs were handy.

I had a place to sit and to read, or write in what was the girls' old school room and nursery. In winter I curled up on a big sofa with a little electric fire for warmth! Sometimes I was invited to the family sitting room (not the little used drawing room full of Chinese furnishing and draperies) to play chess with Mrs Champernowne.

I enjoyed my meals in the big dining room – only breakfast in the kitchen – served by Tom the ex-naval servant.

On summer afternoons we sometimes helped to clear the shrubbery, which had winding paths down to the road. Roland helped too with this work and we had a few chats and laughs together. Enough I think to make Mrs C a little worried about my sharing the cottage accommodation! So she made an offer for me to have a bedroom (the sort a maid would have had) in the house! It was better being near the bathroom and had a comfortable divan bed.

I had the experience of a 'posh' naval ball at Admiralty House, Devonport! When Daphne asked me to go, I sent home for my long evening dress, and asked Lill and Ethel to make me a black velvet cape! This they did and I used it for many years – it had squared shoulders, a metal clasp and was lined with white silk. This showed that Lill still hastened to grant any of my requests!

The blue dress of taffeta had big puff sleeves and buttoned effect from neck to hem. I had worn it a few times for small dances, which I went to with John Woolley, Pam and her art student friends.

Incidentally while sitting on the 'schoolroom sofa' in leisure time, I wrote long letters to John Woolley giving our life history to each other up to and after we met! Very romantic, but nothing came of it. I never had copies as he kept them. After I told him about Jack, I never heard from him again!

The naval ball was certainly grand, and one of the last to have 'programmes' for the dancing. Little folded white cards with loop to go round one's wrist and a pencil attached by a cord. One was supposed to write in partner's names that had booked a dance! Needless to say I didn't have many, but enjoyed it all!

Daphne took me on my one and only visit to Plymouth to do Christmas shopping. It was cheap and easy to post presents and I earned fifteen shillings per week! Daphne had persuaded me to buy tweed in a lovely green-grey colour and had a suit made by her dressmaker.

I don't remember much of Christmas, my first away from home. Betty came and we sat in the "Chinese" room on Christmas Day and Betty played the piano and sang beautifully "These Foolish Things".

We also went to a neighbours' house for a party, but memory is vague.

Boxing Day was hunting, of course, and back to work.

I do remember a lovely summer picnic by the river with a group including Roland, and a boy who used to ride Daphne's show ponies. They did some shooting at targets on the picnic and I was shown how to use a gun.

The two shows I recall are the "Devon County" and the "Bath and West" – both big shows and I enjoyed being 'groom' for winning ponies.

Daphne had a lot of back trouble – the result I was told of a bad fall sometime before. On hunting days I went in the car with Mrs C to 'follow' and to take the trailer.

The summer passed pleasantly, but war clouds were gathering and I went home for an unpaid holiday while the Champernownes went up to Scotland salmon fishing.

WAR AND I MOVED TO MANOR HOUSE, FRAISTHORPE.

When September 2nd came Mother said I shouldn't go back to Devon – "We don't know what will happen". So I wrote to "Vineyard" and my trunk was packed and sent by rail. As I'd seen Jack during the holiday, I went by bus to Fraisthorpe to see if I could be a land girl.

The weather was glorious I remember and harvest going well. Mrs Megginson was the boss it seemed and said, "Well you can come - but we can't pay you – meat for work". I said, "Yes" and went back to collect my clothes!

I had jodhpurs, boots and my stable overalls, so soon got to work – stooking and 'picking' on the stack. I loved it, also the big baskets of 'lowances' sent out to the field. I even had a special bottle of tea, as the large enamel can for all the others was sweetened!

I had a big bed – mahogany with 'half-tester' headboard, in a front bedroom looking across the fields to the sea.

The Harvest Festival in the little "Chapel of Ease" was a big event with all pews full, and Mrs Megginson playing the harmonium. Supper at the Hydes (it was a Friday evening service) was a great social gathering with some of the 'Fred Hyde' family too.

There was a telephone now in the Hydes farmhouse, The Lodge, because of air-raid precautions and the Home Guard was formed. Jack was issued with an unattractive uniform.

Harry Hyde (Henry's father) was a character that never got over the loss of his dear wife Florrie at an early age. His unmarried sister Betsey became his housekeeper and looked after Henry. Brother Fred Hyde and his wife always called "Mrs Fred" had four daughters and a son and were frequent visitors, but with travel restrictions, rations etc they came less in the war years as living in Leeds.

Later in the war we were sad to hear of the death of "Sonny" the only boy in the family. He served in the Navy and drowned in an accident when swimming. He had 'got on well' with cousin Henry, and with Jack on visits to The Lodge.

We worked long hours all that hot September getting in the harvest, to be followed by much "leading" and ploughing before the corn sowing.

I was proud to try the odd half day behind a plough with Tinker and Bonnie. Not an easy job and Jack kept an eye on me to see I kept straight and didn't let Tinker turn short at the end of each furrow.

Jack's sister, Chris was helping her mother in the house and had quite a persistent cough. She was friendly with Henry, "courting" as it was called in far off days. A fact which seemed to worry Mrs Megginson and I wondered whether the friendship was approved of. One evening it was decided that Henry should drive Christine and her mother to visit Dr Leonard Watson in Bridlington as the coughing fits seemed to get worse. They came back, very distressed, as the Doctor appeared worried and told them that Chris must go straight to bed, have complete rest, and not even brush her own hair. "Advanced T.B." and a serious situation was diagnosed. I remember that evening so well, and Jack and I, by then very fond of each other hugged each other, while I wept on his shoulder. Poor Mrs Meg had to become a nurse and kept a fire going in the little grate in that big front bedroom opposite mine.

I was called on to take over household jobs, of which I was quite ignorant, having left Lill to do anything domestic! Apart from feeding hens and mucking out their houses, bringing in the eggs and washing them if necessary, I turned my hand to sweeping, dusting, washing up and easy cooking.

There was, of course, no electricity, so all jobs were laborious and I had done some ironing at home, but with an electric iron. Flat irons heating on the bars of the coal-fired range were most unsatisfactory!

In between sick room duties there was the constant baking to be done. Two long days each week, Tuesdays and Fridays, so Mrs Meg fitted in all that too, and washday was long and hard using the 'copper' and dolly stick and zinc tub with a wooden tub set up on the back-kitchen sink for scrubbing. On wet days, after mangling, clothes and bedding were dried on the overhead rack and aired most of the week.

I was taught to make bread, using a large earthenware bowl with a glazed yellow lining. Seven loaves were needed as a lot of bread was eaten and there were, of course, two men "living in". They used the bedroom above the kitchen, and the back staircase, which also led through to the main landing. The men ate in a little back room, and had an oil stove in cold weather.

When it was not in use for laundry purposes, I filled the copper and lit the fire underneath to boil potatoes for the pigs. They were 'condemned' and died purple so not eaten by humans!

I also learned to skin rabbits and hares, and to pluck and draw chickens.

Each day had regular jobs and routine strictly adhered to, but Wednesday afternoons were more 'free' when one could perhaps go to 'Brid' on the bus to shop, or to sit and tackle some mending of which there was always a pile.

The war was at the 'phoney' stage and not much news in that area. We had an oldish 'wireless' with batteries or 'accumulators' to keep it going.

Jack and I sat in the dining room in the cold evenings with coal fires and oil lamp. Joan taught me on one of her visits to make patchwork for cushions and I enjoyed this work while listening to those good old programmes – Tommy Handley – to make us laugh, or the well known dance bands' music. Joan was working as a land girl then near Beverley.

All the popular songs, from 'Run Rabbit Run' (a skit on Hitler) to 'These foolish things', 'Too much in love to say goodnight', 'Be sure its true when you say I love you because it's a sin to tell a lie', or comic types like 'All by yourself in the moonlight' were still popular. At least they had words one remembers and not the meaningless noisy tunes of the pop music era!

Food rationing meant we had cocoa before bedtime and Jack swore he would never drink it again after the war. We were much better off in the country, and especially on the farm, for food supplies than townsfolk.

I must have had the odd 'day out' to go by bus to Hull, as I remember calling to see mother at the shop, still in Waterworks Street, and very busy after meat rationing, or to meet a friend.

We were restricted with taking the shared car far because of petrol rationing, but Jack and Henry never argued about the use of the little Morris Minor.

On Saturday nights we usually went to the pictures and enjoyed films in Brid. Brid seemed dark and dreary in the blackout, but sometimes we were early enough to do a little shopping before the film. Our needs were little, as vans called at the farm on a regular basis. Bernard Stride, the butcher, twice a week, and Mr Knott the grocer came once a fortnight for the order followed the next day by the delivery van with a huge pile of groceries with one stone sacks of flour, jam in big stone jars for cooking, as the home made kind was used at the table and big bags of dried fruit.

Soap ('Sunlight' or 'Lifebuoy') came in bars and a lot of washing soda, which was hard on the hands and used as detergents would be today. We washed up in a large, deep zinc bowl and drained the pots on a big tin tray – all set out on the kitchen table. That is, the scrubbed one where baking was done. The other table near the window was mahogany, protected in the daytime by a velvet-like cloth and at meal times by the usual tablecloth – usually white with a coloured border.

We were always careful with cleaning materials and during the war when Vim tins (scouring powder) had only the indents of holes in the top to save labour we had to use a nail and hammer to open them up. Pans (blackened from the fire) were scoured on a board in the stone sink in the back kitchen. On Mrs Meg's instructions I only punched out half the holes 'so it will last longer'. That type of economy has lasted all my life and I can't bear a sink to be full of Fairy Liquid bubbles. A little is sufficient!

Old sheets were usually turned "sides to middle" when they became worn and old bits of sheets were machined round the edges to become drying up cloths.

Shirt collars were always 'turned' when showing signs of wear, I did that for Jack's shirts all his life – 'best' then became 'working', but I never turned sheets!

At Manor Farm there was just one large dairy – in the old days before the Milk Marketing Board the separator stood in here – the milk was poured into a 'sile' fixed over the large bowl by crossed pieces of wood called a 'brig' or 'briggs' – tubes then were directed into buckets for cream or separated milk. Any milk not put through the separator was called 'new' milk.

A large wooden bin held the flour – we added baking powder rather than buying self-raising, which cost more.

There were three shelves along the walls, and on the middle one were plate pies, baked twice weekly, and served not only for 'lowances', but for meals too. The men's table always had a pie for breakfast time too! I think the idea was they never left the table feeling empty, as there was always pie to fill up on. They were seldom given bread and jam.

The shelves were lined with neatly folded newspapers, and changed frequently – cakes, buns and small pastries were stored in tins. Meat dishes, either uncooked or cooked were covered with fine wire covers, but flies still found their way to lay their eggs. If this was noticed you washed the joint in vinegar if uncooked - if cooked a dab or two with a vinegar cloth solved the problem, with pies a piece cut off and discarded as if a mouse nibbled pie crust!! Yet stomach upsets were rare, probably we all built up a resistance to germs! Bread was kept in a deep crock called a pancheon and covered with a teacloth. The top shelves had rows of homemade jam, marmalade and pickles.

I remember a large glass container in which eggs were preserved in a solution called Isinglass. Farm eggs were more plentiful in the spring and summer, so when a surplus meant more than needed, they were "put down". This type of egg was only used in cooking, not for boiling, poaching, frying or scrambling. We never made omelettes, but ate a lot of eggs in other ways.

All the time leading up to Christmas, Chris stayed in bed. I think she read, sewed or did some knitting. We would visit and sit by her fire and

Henry went up there too. She had different table ware – kept separate and Mrs Meg toiled up and down with 'slops' which she disposed of in a hole dug in the shrubbery in the front garden, as well as carrying coal for the fire and ashes down each morning. Dr. Watson called when in the village. I don't remember much about that first Christmas of the war. It was all very low key though I was given a stocking on Christmas morning as I'd told Mrs Meg I'd always had one at home. Jack gave me a little gold chain with an aquamarine pedant. I don't know what I gave him!

I did help to pluck and draw poultry and we had a goose for Christmas day and plum pudding, of course. I think we must have gone to Hull too, as Mother and Lill were still living in Park Avenue.

By my 21st birthday in March 1940, Jack and I became officially engaged, and we went to Park Avenue for tea, and to choose a ring from a selection Mother brought 'on approval' from Elvins the Jewellers – I was too shy to go to the shop with Jack! He'd told Mother he could afford £25 and I chose a little diamond with tiny stones around it making a square shape. Afterwards, in the evening, we went to the Little Theatre to see the popular musical "White Horse Inn". I was never keen about wearing a ring and over the years wore mine less and less. Quite recently I gave it to Maureen and I'm pleased to see she wears it often rather than the much more valuable one she inherited from her Auntie Lallie.

Mrs Meg was at first quite off-hand about our engagement, and made no fuss, or took little interest in presents given, or letters of congratulation. People in those days didn't go 'over the top' on such occasions, but her indifference had me in tears at the time. I did hear of her having said to someone "I don't know how she'll come on as a farmer's wife, she can't even knit a sock". As it happens I still haven't knitted a sock, but when Jack needed them Lill kept him well supplied!

Dorothy, however, was enthusiastic, and when we drove over to Park Farm Habton where Ted had the tenancy, she told me to take no notice of Mother and she would help me in getting things together for when we got a farm of our own.

I was given £5 from someone, and chose at Carmichaels a lovely 12 of everything tea service in Wedgewood. Such a dainty design and a pigskin covered low fireside stool with a hunting scene painted on top. I thought it the most beautiful thing ever, and still have it though the hunting scene has faded over the years. That also cost £5.

The tea service has lasted well, only cups have been broken and I replaced those in my china-painting period.

Life continued much the same with housework and spring-cleaning too, when I learned to use a white wash brush. Oil lamps and candles caused sooty ceilings and the dairy walls were done every year.

All drawers were pulled out and swept behind and tidied with fresh lining paper – if you used newspaper the date was a giveaway if not renewed annually! Cupboards and wardrobes were emptied, contents looked at for signs of moth, and items put in the sun to air if they felt damp.

Beds were difficult with spring mattresses – the metal springs needed dusting well, the covers were shaken out or washed. Under mattresses brushed well after turning and featherbeds well shaken and covers washed. Such 'beds' meant shaking feathers well, on a daily basis, otherwise lumps appeared.

The farm men had a mattress, wool mostly, on a bed with wooden slats like the ones popular today.

Blankets were washed on good drying days in summer, just 'poshed' in suds, and put through the mangle.

Carpets were taken up and we heaved them onto the lawn, to be well-shaken and beaten with sticks when the men came in at dinnertime! How the dust flew! Stair carpets came up too, as they were never fitted but kept in place by rods on each step. The sides of the stairs were usually stained dark brown, like the surrounds of rooms with carpets and always took a lot of dusting.

We never used mops, but scrubbed on our hands and knees. Mrs Meg took great pride in the result of all this hard work. She liked things to look 'as white as driven snow' or when polishing 'By it looks as bright as a bullace' (a dark small plum).

Carpets were usually rather thin, no deep piles and when even older and more threadbare they were used in bedrooms. Curtains were thin, unlined, and I never remember any being replaced! When Mrs Meg moved to Manor House in 1933, new flowered cretonne curtains in rather dull colours were made the same for all windows.

There was very little in that house that I admired – only the mahogany Davenport desk tucked away in the back bedroom. In those days the farmer would choose a bedroom nearest the buildings so he could hear if anything was wrong with stock in the night! The best bedroom was rarely used by family other than in illness, and was kept smarter than the others. I heard that visitors always took their coats up, to leave on the bed or for ladies to make use of the po or commode.

I must admit, this way of life, and housework and cooking was quite new to me especially as I look back now, and wonder how we managed with a 3 seater privy (2 in one and one singular) down the garden path!

Cold and dark too on winter mornings and nights.

Baths meant 'pumping up' for twenty minutes in the back kitchen to get enough water to the bathroom so not frequent and, of course, I missed all electric gadgets as well as light. I still don't take to the present trend to light candles, and to use oil lamps, or reproductions adapted to electricity!

It's strange how fashions change – and no one would have thought of cornice poles being used again after the invention of what we called "railway tracks", or even the expanding metal rods. As to marble fireplaces, washstands, cast iron bedroom fire surrounds, we couldn't get rid of them quickly enough!

I've written before of farm horses and all the seasonal work. Jack did most of his shepherding jobs in summer evenings and I loved to go round with him. We had a pony called Flash, but I disliked the name and called her 'Porny' and liked to ride in the evenings.

I loved the summer evenings, going round the farm with Jack, and took a great interest in sheep, horses, cows, and the growing crops.

The fears of invasion made changes on the beach, and down Hydes fields. Tank traps, stone posts in and around fields, barbed wire on the beach itself and concrete 'look out' posts. Even the half-a-cottage, the only remaining part of Auburn village, lost to the sea many years before, had been blown up as seen as a landmark.

By June, Jack and I decided on marriage as we heard there was a possibility of some people being moved further inland if the dreaded invasion came. Dunkirk had been a tragedy and now Fraisthorpe village was full of army personnel. Some camped in paddocks and beds appeared in barns. There were soldiers all around, sentries with fixed bayonets "Who goes there?" – a curfew at night, and restrictions on travel from anyone coming within five miles of the coast.

With fear of being parted, if I as a single unattached person was made to leave the area, we arranged a small wedding in Barmston Church for July 25th 1940. I shall avoid much repetition if I write briefly of this very important day as I've described the wedding, honeymoon, clothes, and gifts in my other books. So enough to say, it was all wonderful in difficult circumstances, and I was delighted to become Mrs Jack Megginson.

I'll now call my mother-in-law Nellie in this book and once we were married she accepted me in the family and I hope I became a satisfactory daughter-in-law!

At the time of our wedding, Chris had been sent to Fairfield Sanatorium in York, and visiting was quite difficult. Mostly Uncle J.O. (see other books) drove Nellie to visit about once a week. Jack and I only went once after she'd had an operation for collapsing the worst affected lung. We were sad to see Chris in a ward of young girls looking even more poorly. When she came home, to have a bed in the drawing room, Jack and I bought her a very smart blue portable radio, up-to-date and much nicer than the usual wartime models. There was a slight improvement when she had a few outings, and went to buy a new coat.

It's hard to recall the rest of that year when we lived at Manor House. We had refurbished our bedroom a bit, and my school friend Joan helped with that, and was a frequent visitor as working on the land in East Yorkshire.

Mother and Lill had moved out of Hull when air raids got bad, and the shop got a direct hit. For a time they had rooms at a farm in Withernwick – Mother travelled to new shop premises by train, and Lill found it difficult living with people rather than having her own way of running a house.

I remember Mother being puzzled one Autumn Sunday to be told "we can't use the front room and light a fire to-day, because we are going brambling on Tuesday" I can see her landlady's reasoning as using a sitting room would mean cleaning it up after the fire – sweeping and dusting. No time on Mondays, which were always hard, work with washing and ironing. Tuesday when the room could have been cleaned, must leave time to go into the fields to pick blackberries or locally – brambles.

After that period Mother and Lill moved to Hornsea for about a year I think, into part of Joan's parents' lovely house in Burton Road. The furniture from Park Avenue had been put in store, Lill again was unhappy, and for a few days when so ill with depression that she went to stay with her relation Ethel. Jack agreed to let me go to Hornsea for a few days to look after Mother. Lill returned, but not happy till in a house again.

It was strange to be living in separate quarters to Joan's parents in a house where I'd visited a lot in school days. I think our presence prevented evacuees being billeted there.

Poor Chris died in May 1941, and it was my first experience of helping to deal with the aftermath of a family death. Nellie relied on me to telephone relatives – using the only phone in the village.

I also went with Nellie to buy mourning clothes and was surprised by the corpse being "laid out" in her coffin of prettily lined satin, and left in the best bedroom for friends and neighbours to "pay their respects".

A great many of the Megginson and Sykes families assembled for the funeral at Carnaby Church and in spite of the sadness of the occasion I was glad to meet so many nice relations at Manor House afterwards.

The war had really moved nearer and we often saw the blaze of fires over Hull and heard the planes overhead, but apart from the aerial battle over Fraisthorpe when a German plane was brought down (more in other books) we had few nearby frights.

Later that summer we had two couples of Army officers with their wives billeted on us. I think it was a good distraction for Mrs Meg. Captain Guy Turner and Captain Brian Turner. Although brothers in the same regiment, they were not at all alike. The" Guys" were a more quiet, serious pair. She came from Norfolk and I remember liked to boil sausages in milk with onions! The "Brian" couple were more relaxed and lively and she (I forget the wives' names) came from Sussex and put lovely looking family photos in their bedroom and I much admired her parents' home, very elegant with large garden. I think her name was Helen, as I can see it now engraved on the leather writing case – blue – lying on the chest of drawers.

They had the 'best' bedroom, and the "Guys" one at the back which Mr and Mrs Meg vacated in the bombing. He had a bed in the old 'office' used by Uncle J.O. when he lodged with them, and she had a camp bed put up in the passage between kitchen and hall. Probably the safest place as no windows!

The Turner brothers seemed to share a batman who helped in various ways and spent hours polishing their shoes in the back kitchen, pressing a finger into the polish and using a circular motion, achieved a mirror like surface on the toe caps!

I cleaned the bedrooms and two downstairs rooms. I really can't imagine how we managed for baths and the outside loo. Perhaps they used Army facilities? Someone did their laundry too, and helped with some of their cooking.

Clothes were not changed frequently as in later years of that century. Fabrics were not "easy care" and even hand washing not simple as today.

I've written very little of Mr Meg, but although a more quiet character than his wife, I think he suffered from her 'nagging' streak where he was concerned. A fact that had worried Jack in his younger years, and he longed for a loving and more caring devotion in his wife, and I do hope he got it!

Harold Meggingson was a kind, I would think 'jovial' type in his youth. No doubt, the hard-up years of marriage after a more affluent start brought a strain between them, and money 'wasted' in the years when drinking and card playing evenings were popular with the local farmers – annoyed Nellie very much. I got the feeling that all the many relations felt compassion for Harold.

The period of the officers and wives living with us didn't last long as fears of invasion faded, and the 'troops' left the village, although the coast was still guarded. I found the Turner wives a welcome change of conversation in the brief times when we had a chance to chat.

I've already written in detail of the war restrictions, rationing, and 'make do and mend' – also of our plans to move to South Kingsfield, the following spring. The summer evenings meant we didn't miss our sitting room. Jack and I longed for a place of our own, but the first sight of the dilapidated, unattractive, featureless house nearly made me cry! Jack cheered me up and I hoped I could cope with living in such squalid circumstances.

Dorothy was a help in storing up household goods, and Jack and I shopped for necessary cutlery and kitchenware at Woolworths on Saturdays! I still use cake tins bought for sixpence, and odd bits of china have survived from Fraisthorpe years!

WE BECOME TENANTS OF SOUTH KINGSFIELD

I certainly enjoyed planning schemes to make the best of the old shabby house, and Mother helped a lot too, with paying for our bargain purchase of a 'bombed out' carpet, and large bright rugs from a store in Hull. She also knew a shop manager well at Willis's (now Alders) who supplied coupon-free fabric for curtains. In my younger days dresses had been 'run up' by Mother and Lill from materials from this man known as "Mac" at low prices.

In spite of all the hard work to get rid of filth, beetles, mice, to scrub paint before painting and general state of chaos, the reward of seeing a gradual transformation, even with second hand stuff was great.

I loved 'setting out' my things, although the two living rooms had to wait for new fireplaces before any decorating could be done. All this time Jack and Charlie, the live-in lads, had to be well fed promptly for meals, 'lowances', beds changed, all with inadequate equipment! Charlie was older, and had worked for the previous tenants.

It was then the fashion to paint kitchen furniture bright blue, at least cupboards, small tables, dressers, and even storage tins. As regards wallpaper and shades of paint, we were still in the 'all cream era'. The local decorator did the three good-sized bedrooms and staircase.

Joan came for a weekend soon after we moved in April 1942, and we spent a lot of time painting the back kitchen, which soon had a new sink and taps instead of pumps! There was an ancient black wall-oven in there, but I found it didn't work well, and the black leaded range was seldom lit as it had a messy grate with a pit under it to collect ash. Eventually I got it boarded over to save dust and dirt. Now it would be considered a 'feature' and preserved.

Thinking back to 'teenage' years, a term not known in far off days, I must have been lacking in maturity as regards SEX! My older sisters had had various boyfriends from quite an early age, especially Olive who was 'mad about the boys' even as a schoolgirl. I felt it all rather stupid as I did about all forms of 'growing up' and having no serious relationship before Jack – it was all quite an experience for this late developer!

It is hard to imagine now, in 2005, how blatant attitudes of today would have been very much frowned on in 1940's. Magazines were puritan in content, and no books on such a personal matter available. I'm sure this under-cover approach was very wrong, but the aftermath of Victorian and Edwardian morals still lingered.

Birth control was never discussed in public, and illegitimate births severely frowned on, and often concealed with babies being adopted. A single mother would have had a hard life.

When I discovered I was pregnant in the late spring after the move to Kingsfield it was quite a shock (good luck rather than good management why this state had not occurred earlier!) and I was totally embarrassed.

Talking of this to a young mother today, I was expressing revulsion at the photos of a pregnant 'celeb' in a state of undress. "I could never have imagined this" I said and the reply was "But we are all proud to show off a bump" And they certainly do!

So different from poor, shy Irene – but all that part is also in "Mud on my Doorstep" and I did have lots of help from Mother-in-law, Mother, Lill and friends. Though during the war only Joan was near, visiting was difficult, and although I wrote a lot of letters in limited spare time, there were no telephone conversations.

Dear Mother had rented a little detached house in St. James Road, Bridlington- so she and Lill were much happier. Mother went by train to the shop and Lill came by bus, twice a week to help me with washing and baking. Nellie helped in many ways when needed. The estate put in a bathroom, but no loo – so we bought a "chemical closet" installed in bathroom!

On dreaded threshing days, I would go up to help her at Manor House. I rode a bike or walked the mile to the village.

I tried to 'carry-on-regardless' about being pregnant, then called 'expecting' and unlike today there were no ante-natal clinics, which I'd have hated in any case. I saw our dear Doctor by the time I was about four months. I went with kidney pains and managed to say, "I think I may be expecting a baby". So he examined me, said I shouldn't have difficulty over the birth and told me it was time I booked in at "The Avenue" where everyone went! So that was that! I may have had another examination, but I hadn't any more kidney infections, so didn't bother. I really disliked being pregnant in spite of feeling well. It certainly wasn't a thrill (as in today's young mums) to feel baby movements, and I hated the clothes thought to conceal one's shape.

Our first harvest came, and went, Charlie still using Sharper, our first horse, we had one or two others, but a tractor soon took over to pull the old binder which Uncle Edward at Towthorpe gave Jack.

I helped with poultry, but mostly worked in the house all day. Uncle Jack came regularly to do the veg garden, fruit bushes and his beehives.

We still didn't have an everyday sitting room, as that room which one had to walk through to the staircase (no hall) still needed the new fireplace. The far sitting room had Mother's old 3-piece suite from Hull and carpet bought second hand. Linen covers were made for the plush suite, now rather moth eaten from being in store, by an old lady who lived over the harbour in Brid. I was so proud of the covers with a pattern featuring figures in a rural landscape. We never went through in evenings to sit in that comfortable room when winter nights came, but I had to 'make do' with the horse hair chaise-longue which Jack had bought at a farm sale for two pounds. I'd tacked on a cover of tapestry type material and even edged it with braid, but it still felt rather prickly from the horsehair underneath.

Jack would doze while listening to the wireless, and Charlie sometimes joined us before going to his bed up the back stairs. There was a Windsor chair I'd got in a ten bob lot from the blacksmith, otherwise just a mixture of dining chairs in plain wood and a rocking chair bought from Joan's father. Another ten bob!

One can't compare prices now inflation and decimal coinage has taken over, but that chair still at Cot Nab is worth quite a lot!

When time came for the evening milking Jack was often asleep in his chair and I had difficulty in waking him! Jack milked three times a day, and John Barnby came from the village to help. The cheque from the Milk Marketing Board was a regular income and he was proud of his pedigree Friesian herd. We had to keep records of calves, at least the female ones, and I did the job of filling in the correct black and white markings for identification.

I think Christmas was still 'low-key' in 1942, but Uncle J.O. brought us a little Christmas tree, and I had a job to find things to hang on it! I'm sure we would join our families for meals and I, heavily pregnant, was thankful to make a fire in the sitting room and have that luxury for two days. It was difficult to keep the room warm enough when fires were infrequent, and I remember putting cushions on the hearthrug to air by the fire. The under-stairs cupboard was in that room, but no use for storing anything as affected by damp.

The silver candlesticks from my in-laws had pride of place on the tiled fireplace. That period of fire surrounds was thought lovely at the time, but hideous, years later! The one the estate men were installing the day I went into labour with Tony was one of the nicest in that type, and I was so pleased with it. Tenants accepted what came!

This reader must look to "Mud on my doorstep" or "A life on the Wolds" to learn more of Tony's birth on January 19th 1943.

Being ignorant about giving birth, I had only cows to go by, and I didn't follow that example as anticipated. Drama indeed! With Jack, Uncle J. O. and Mother-in-law at York market to sell a cow, I was bewildered, and miserable. Jack had gone the night before, to be ready in good time, for this important sale, or he might have known why things were happening as they did.

I made bread, put it in the oven, and then felt so sick and ill I went up to bed to avoid the workmen in the room we would call 'the nursery'. Now it would be 'playroom'!

I won't repeat from my first book about sending John, the cowman on his bike, to the village to get help, and Henry Hyde drove me to Brid, but Tony arrived quickly after getting to the Avenue when I still wondered if this strange process was really having a baby! I was even more surprised to find I felt perfectly well straight afterwards and hungry. I thought I'd feel frail and an invalid, as I'd read about in novels!

I had one awful midwife, and one kind and sweet, and 'Dear Doctor' arrived in time! This is all exclamation marks, but I was so staggered by everything it really needs a row of them. Jack was given the message when he returned home, and quickly came to see me. I'd have hated to have him around before it was all over and in any case he wouldn't have been allowed in. Even so he didn't even see Tony through the glass door as no visitors could pick up the babies. He said he'd wait to pick him up himself and spend more visiting time with me. The other good news of the day was the cow made £112, and I'd been promised anything over

£100. A fortune indeed! Babies were only brought to bed-bound Mums for feeding times, so I had two weeks of being able to rest, write and read and eat meals provided for me in my private room. I got very weepy one day, realising this rest period must end soon; I'd have to learn how to bath and to deal with a baby's nappies. (These lessons began at 10 days) and I began to feel I would never fit it all in between all the regular daily round of meals, housework, washday etc. However, it was winter and easier for Jack to help with Tony. Though naturally capable with babies, and little children, he wasn't inclined to household jobs.

Parents to-day choose just when to have babies, and gone are the 'four hourly' feeds, the constant nappy washing by hand, and the forgetting about the baby for three or hour hours at a time! Also the advice given by "dear Doctor" hold him out after every feed, even over a little bowl – it will become a reflex habit, and save a lot of nappies, as indeed it did.

Now potty training starts at over two years old! We would have been ashamed to have a walking child in nappies, even if we had pools sometimes and little towelling pants to change.

Babies stayed out in prams in all weathers, other than fog. For rain we had a porch over the front door. Mother gave me the "Mothercraft Manual" and I followed instructions, but when Tony was five months sister Olive came, and said I must start giving him Robinsons groats! That meant I had to buy a double pan and stir over the fire for ten minutes! Incidentally I still use those two pans. I used a cup and spoon and the change of diet from breast milk was welcomed. I never bought a bottle in five years of babies and felt this a great advantage – certainly no dummies either!

We had some disturbed nights, of course, when babies were young, but one could resort to pulling them from cot to bed and trying not to fall asleep till placed back in the cradle.

Recently I read of the total cost of bringing up a child till school age and it mounted up to thousands of pounds! Apart from nappy material, home made vyella nighties and bought vests, we had few expenses. Lill found a second hand pram in Bridlington. Mother knitted shawls and 'matinee coats' (what a strange name for little cardigans). Bootees and bibs made present from friends and relations – also pillow-cases (who ever would give pillows now, and full of feathers too?)

A bath on a stand with shelf underneath was given from Auntie Muriel and the 'treasure cot' newly draped. Later we bought a new drop-sided one, but a low-chair was borrowed and a wooden rocking horse-cum-chair at ground level was popular and called 'Rocker'.

There were no little carrying chairs, or the sort that tilted for a new baby to rest in. If not lying flat we propped them up in a chair with arms, and wedged with cushions. In a farmhouse there was room for the big pram to come indoors, and Olive gave me a pink carry-cot, but we seldom took a baby long distances. There was no thought of not nursing a baby on car journeys, and farmers' wives didn't expect to have time to go out often, and if they did one would have to have friends, or families to come and 'sit in'. I never had a paid sitter, so another expense saved.

After nightgowns in the first six weeks little silky rompers were worn by Tony and the girls who came later had dresses. Pretty, and often smocked, or embroidered, the only difference between rompers and dresses being the rompers had elastic gathers and a buttoned strap between the legs. To keep warm they would have blankets or shawls.

By the time we had two babies, we had a phone installed, Jack not thinking it really necessary, but once we had it he used it a lot.

I'm still amazed by some of the clothes worn by tiny great-grandchildren – so sensible and easy-care and masses of them. Such variety of colours too. Navy for new babies! Who would have thought it?

Yet to-day's babies and toddlers take up far more time to look after than those kept to the regime of the 'forties! Were we cruel and uncaring? I don't think so, and there were no 'nurseries' or play schools, but in spite of being busy housebound Mums we were always there!

Time to spend with little ones was limited, but in the middle of baking or cleaning I'd stop to dress a doll, solve a puzzle, or sort out a quarrel. I also feel that children given too many treats and toys will, perhaps grow up expecting life to be too easy with less ability to face up to troubles. This attitude has probably been the case through many generations, but never has so much, in a material sense, been available from birth to adult status.

Now they think they are grown up from the age of ten, and a great deal of innocent joys in childhood have been lost.

The pill, of course, made all the difference for a planned family, and sometimes now having a baby is suddenly a last minute thought before time runs out. That wasn't the case in our life in South Kingsfield days. After Tony, came Jennifer, Maureen and Rachel in less than five years and before I was thirty. So we really felt the Doctor's advice should be sought and taken. I joked, "with all this expense, we'll have to reserve sex for special celebrations", but Rachel proved to be our last baby. I was glad later that the family were near together and good companions.

Domestic work got a bit easier with the calor-gas stove, two rings and a grill. A haircord carpet on the birch floor of the kitchen meant less floor washing, and a kinder surface for children's knees, especially when crawling, but I did sew some simple dungarees! I made pinnies for the girls to wear over their cotton dresses, which had puffed sleeves and gathered waists. This saved washing piling up and difficult ironing too.   In winter the same type of dresses in vyella, mostly made by Nellie's friend Miss Hall, a resident seamstress who would stay in people's homes to make new clothes, mend sheets, run up curtains, or transform old into new by 'cutting down or turning'. In our case Miss Hall stayed with Nellie, and her charge was very low.

Mother knitted cardigans (or pullovers for Tony) and the worst clothes to deal with were the leggings, which matched little overcoats. Quite smart in tweedy material they had elastic waistbands, but fastened below the knee with a row of buttons!

I was glad when they got beyond that stage and loved to see them in winter outfits of tailored coats with velvet collars. Trousers for girls were not thought of, though when they started riding ponies, we sent away for jodhpurs from the Caldene Clothing Company.

After Rachel was walking Jack bought a Cairn puppy (Nellie would never have had a dog indoors) and after that we were never without a dog in the house. A pony was bought for Tony, but he showed no interest whatever when it hadn't an engine, but Jennifer, Maureen and Rachel all loved those ponies. Jack bought a horse for himself, and when I'd ceased having babies, I too started riding again in limited free time.

But enough of that, I've already written in detail of that side of family life.

Looking back I'm amazed that so many friends came to visit after the restrictions of travel in wartime were lifted. Without electricity or sanitation other than the wretched ELSAN in the bathroom it's surprising that they could endure the primitive life to be with us! Yet diaries and photo albums record them all.

Electricity came with a generator, mainly for farm use, and a milking machine! Life got much easier when Mother bought an electric washing machine, so Jack could take our laundry to Bridlington, and collect it later!

We started going to dances, dinners, and to the theatre, but not to restaurants, or hotels for meals. If we went out for a day in the car we always took a picnic, also when going down to the beach.

The high spots of the Fraisthorpe years are, looking back, beach picnics, teaching the girls to swim in the sea (Tony not so keen) riding on the sands for miles, visiting the Towthorpe Megginsons for tea, and taking family, and friends for long drives in the car.

Holidays were few, but the long car journey was worth it to stay in Wiltshire with Ellis and Margery, and once we had a brief farmhouse holiday in the Lake District.

Sometimes I went off on a train to see old friends. When Nellie took over the children for a few days there was a list for good and bad behaviour with the chance of black marks! Father-in-law had died when Jennifer was a baby and Nellie now lived at Bessingby.

I look back to dampness and the ever present problem of damp patches on walls, the musty smell of the fireside cupboards in the nursery, and the fact that we kept all the children's clothes in the big old wardrobe in the kitchen, as the only place were they could be kept 'aired'.

That wardrobe I've written about before, but for the record it is still in use in the 'office' at Cot Nab. When I was a child my Mother bought it from a neighbour whose mother had had it specially built for her clothes, books, toys and even a deep drawer for hats! It isn't made of any specific wood, originally grained, and varnished to look like walnut. I painted it in cream for the kitchen when Mother passed it on to me. The mouldings of cupboards and drawers were picked out in red. Moving to Cot Nab kitchen where damp was not a problem, though no central heating, I changed the colour to panels of pale green on cream, and had shelves made for the two tall cupboards for kitchen storage. The children still kept their divided drawers for their treasures.

No units in that kitchen when we lived there. Not long before we left, we had the room re-decorated to a more Victorian feel, and Jack helped me to strip the cupboard of paint and with much hard work hopefully created a pine look. In that state it now remains. A huge piece of joiner-made Victorian workmanship.

I shall never forget the disaster of the aftermath of a prolonged snow period at Fraisthorpe when 4 ceilings fell down through snow accumulation in the roof, which lacked 'under-drawing'. I don't know how we lived through the weeks of chaos and how we kept the girls' beds dry. The spare room was alright, and Tony's little lean-to room. Our bedroom ceiling leaked badly and sagged in the middle, but didn't collapse. We had only Jim living in the men's bedroom at that time and he had to be moved, bed and po, into the sitting room when his ceiling collapsed! The house was all upset till the estate workmen had repaired ceilings, but nothing was done about the actual roof, and it was due to another leaking ceiling that we decided to accept a new tenancy.

Manor House, Fraisthorpe, where Irene & Jack met

Irene aged 14, leading Boxer scruffling turnips

Irene rides 'Porny', Manor House

Jack & Irene Wedding Day, July 25th 1940

Jack on honeymoon

South Kingsfield Farm

Jack in first year of marriage

Irene on honeymoon - still a tomboy!

*South
Kingsfield
Farm*

Tony with pedal car

Jennifer

Maureen with 'plaits'

Rachel

Family & friends among stooks, 1950

Mother & Lill moved to 4 St James Road, Bridlington 1942

1956. THE COT NAB YEARS

It was with such memories of coping with great inconvenience in so many ways, that when the time came to move to Cot Nab I could only rejoice, and revel in a big, dry, light high ceiling house. My spirits were high too, with electricity laid on, two lavatories and views in all directions. Also we had a good landlord – Lord Halifax!

True we faced snow, and fog with winds blowing strongly enough to lift the sitting room carpet in a gale, but we were in a friendly environment, nearer our Megginson relations, and within a pleasant walking distance of a lovely village, if you didn't mind climbing back 600 ft to the highest point of the Wolds.

We were there thirty years and had very happy times in spite of ups and downs of farm prices, family problems, the time given to caring for elderly relations, and the sadness of losing Mother and Lill after distressing deterioration.

Four teenagers didn't mean so many difficulties as that age group seems to bring with it today. We could also forget all the security needed in 2000. When going to bed at one stage, we would leave a list on the kitchen table of the four names if all out, and last one would lock the back door!

Cot Nab saw horse years at their peak – pony clubs, with rallies and camps – hunting, Rachel's eventing, and after her marriage Jack's driving period with Tom and Jerry.

On my part, in my rather hopeless horsemanship, I loved riding, especially through stubble fields, or up and down our pretty lanes, through Givendale – "the gallops" (now out of bounds) or time spent watching Rachel schooling or jumping in paddock or wood.

Summer evenings going round the fields with Jack 'shepherding' or winter evenings keeping warm close to a big fire in the dining room.

On the domestic side, the work must have still been never ending in many ways. The family were growing up, and they didn't get driven frantically to and fro, except where ponies were concerned, but I still did a lot of baking, and entertaining on a low-key level mostly with occasional dining room meals and fireside suppers. Only a basic electric cooker, yet one just managed and it was wonderful after years of the Yorkist Range!

During early Cot Nab years, the three girls were reluctant boarders as no 'comprehensive' then in Pocklington. Tony had joined Martin Stringer in making long journeys by bikes and train to Market Weighton.

The dairy was a short walk from the kitchen, and all fresh food kept there, until the joy of first a fridge, and later a freezer, and neither exactly handy, but we did have a sink in the kitchen after years of carrying pots through to the back kitchen.

As in Fraisthorpe years I still made a great thing of spring cleaning – the kitchen and bathroom at first still had gloss paint on all walls, and these were washed. Mother-in-law came to stay sometimes, and helped me to do paper-hanging, but I soon learned to take on that job and eventually a lot more when the girls married.

For the very high ceilings a lot of paper was needed, and local decorators came in to put on the thirty rolls necessary for hall, staircase and landing. One just kept on during light evenings when the men were working outside, till all was 'done' in the annual clean, reaching up from the top of a pair of steps, or polishing floors on hands and knees.

As I didn't drive, I was at home a lot for cooking, cleaning and gardening. There was always constant baking often with 'lowances' extra, and in any case we always gave the men apple pie or bacon cake every morning. The latter was just slices of bacon in pastry - Jack loved it!

I think the large gangs of potato pickers (all by hand) were the worst to feed twice daily, even more so than harvest time.

Few farms now give workers any 'lowance', and in any case there are few workers. Pack ups are needed at the start of the day, cold drinks as well as hot and crisps, kitkats and sandwiches and little in the way of pies!

A great many farmers' wives in this century need I.T. skills to cope with all the paper work and a lot go out to jobs, or help with some sort of diversification in the difficult years of low profit for the old ways of farming.

It still seems sad to have no stock of any kind at Cot Nab. We had such variety in our early years there. Cows, store cattle, sheep, pigs, hens and ducks.

Now, in townie-style, eggs come in cartons and milk in bottles. No one would thank you today for sides of fat bacon and large hams hanging from ceiling hooks. As to baking a row of pork pies after killing a pig, the art is dying, and I know I'd never get one right now with hot water pastry, and the jelly made from boiling a pig's foot!

Jack loved brawn, and ate it well sprinkled with vinegar and sugar; it's a wonder I ever got out of the kitchen! And after all it was often in winter the warmest place.

One needed a coat in winter to answer the phone in the hall, or to Hoover the bedrooms, and it took courage to leave a warm bed on icy mornings! We kept the bathroom moderately warm after Nellie bought us a Flatly towel drier, which was also in use for drying small articles. The wall heater was high up and needed to be on a long time, and costly, to send out much heat.

The cottage end of the house was useful for a workman and family, then for my mother and Lill in mother's years of illness. After her death Lill lived alone there and was a good help to me. When she became ill and confined to one room we moved her into the main house. After Maureen's divorce she lived in the cottage with her three little girls. Like Mother, Lill stayed with us till she died. When Tony took over he soon had the house back to its original state and installed central heating.

It took Jack and me a long time to find a semi-retirement house after recovering from the shock of Tony's query "when are you going to look for somewhere else to live?" It was true that he, Pam, Jane and Mark needed a bigger house and to be on the farm rather than living at Uncleby. Jack was determined not to move from the area around Bishop Wilton, which he loved so much, and I didn't want to go far away either.

We had eight grand-children within easy reach, and the Cot Nab years, after the marriages had been enriched by the lively little ones, who played together, meeting often and seemingly at times like one big Victorian size family.

Divorce had become more acceptable than in our youth, and although causing, in all cases much sadness, and distress, perhaps was better than years of misery in some families where parents were so unhappy with each other, yet had no alternative than to 'stick it out'.

In Maureen's case, the three little girls who came to live 'next door' in the cottage gave us great joy and when we eventually found we could buy Witton House in Bishop Wilton village, we were thankful when Maureen and the girls were offered the tenancy of a vacant farmhouse on the Garrowby estate at Youlthorpe, near enough to still be within easy reach and we had a nearby paddock and a stable to rent for ponies.

Thinking again of the Cot Nab years, there were many personal memories, especially my increased interest in writing, and the pleasure of painting.

I had always kept up long correspondence with my old school friends and with Margery from Devon years. I'd also written from Kingsfield for the Farmers' Weekly, but never been paid for anything. One unpaid commission was to write a monthly article for the National Farmers' Journal – I saw an appeal by the editor for a 'women's page' as the present writer was giving up. She wrote under an assumed name, and when I heard I could have the job (unpaid) I decided to use Prudence Bailey, which was the name, I chose in schooldays for when I became an actress!

Mickey chose Margaruite Fyffe-Millar, and Pam who fancied a dancing career was to be known as Selina Fairfax! Only Prudence Bailey ever appeared in print.

I enjoyed doing the monthly articles, which I did for a year, and was pleased at Christmas to receive a beautiful bouquet of flowers from the N.F.U local office.

When the 'doing up' of kitchens was all the rage I looked round mine, and wrote "What – No Formica?" and managed to get it accepted for "The Lady". I expected to hear whether it would be used or not, but realised later in life, that an unreturned manuscript is usually accepted. I first knew I was "in print" when the Sloans bought the magazine (probably for holiday accommodation) and read it. Quite a feather in my cap as "The Lady" is known for being quite difficult to get into and I was never lucky with any other offerings. I think I got five pounds.

Later, after we'd had the townie youngsters from Hull to spend the day learning about the farm and countryside – two coaches of them – I sent an account to the magazine "Parent" and called it "The day the children came" another five pounds I think, or perhaps seven pounds.

Still writing as Prudence Bailey I did several articles for "Horse World" on "Mum's view of Pony Club Camp" – same for shows and horse trials and later when Rachel was eventing I got one in "Horse and Hound" Christmas number on "Trials of travelling to Trials", and still went in for competitions in the "Farmers' Weekly" – and once I was third in the Yorkshire Post, winning fifteen pounds.

At one stage I thought I'd learn to type as I usually wrote 'due to lack of typist' as an excuse. I went as far as evening classes in Pocklington, and used the old heavy machine the girls had bought, but I was no good, though I did try to practise.

When Margery in one of fortnightly exchanges of letters wrote 'please don't keep trying to type' I gave up, and have never tried since, ignoring the advantages now a days of word processors and all manner of advance technology.

I still write a rough scribbled copy, then print out carefully by hand. It seems as if I must let the words come down from brain to pen.

I also went in more for painting as a hobby too, and joined a class with Mrs Hobbs in the village. For a time I learned to use oils, and managed a few quite successful paintings of places – but with easel – messy tubes, palette and time for drying, I eventually went back to water colours.

Another interest lasting a few years was china-painting with Mrs Watson, a good teacher who came to the village. I really enjoyed painting plates to hang on walls, or for friends' special occasions I also replaced broken cups from my 21st present service, and did another service with a simple barley design. Eventually I felt all friends and relations had some of my efforts in that line, so gave up. If I'd had a handy kiln, perhaps I'd have done occasional pieces if I felt like it.

My sewing talent is very limited, apart from mending (yes, we always mended or altered things) but I loved dressing dolls and teddies. I did a lot in Kingsfield years, working by poor light on dark winter evenings. I kept up this 'doll standard' dress making for the granddaughters, and also spent hours in winter making things to sell at the church bazaar. Jack had been Warden at St. Edith's for years, and I became Secretary, and still am.

As well as hobby horses, with Jack's help, I did decorated notepads, using birthday cards and fire screens covered with pictures too, varnished when finished. Bazaar years saw peg dolls, and novelty pencils with ping-pong ball tops decorated as funny heads, once it was small teddies, and I even managed a large elephant, big enough for a toddler to sit on. I decorated the elephant Indian style, and raffled it for the bazaar, and then made a similar one for Sarah. I found fur fabric easy to work with, as stitches don't show!

Poor Rachel once said she looked at the stitches showing through the hem of her school skirt and felt quite ashamed of Mum's sewing! She was the most gifted in the family for all forms of needlework (from an early age) dress making, or knitting. She also took to upholstery in married life and tapestry pictures.

I never aspired to exotic cooking, but in Cot Nab years, we did a lot of entertaining with very little in the way of culinary aids. I never felt keen to change to electric mixers, blenders, and even now fear the microwave ovens.

The old big kitchen table, and scrubbed pastry board is looked back on now with regret, at having to manage a good baking session on a kitchen counter with little space for my mess with flour and rolling pin.

We still asked friends for hand round suppers using a trolley, and small tables in the sitting room. The sandwich, sausage roll, cakes and trifle type of meal. More or less routine and not a great effort to produce and little imagination needed!

Tea was most popular at all times before percolators, cafetiere types of coffee machinery became the norm. We would use pretty 'best' china, and teapots with napkins, tea knives (I still have the pear handled set) and sugar bowls with silver tongs, now alas looked upon as out of date and 'old hat'. We did start to go out for the rare evening meal as farmers began to lead what I felt was a more sophisticated life-style, like holidays abroad and smart rather regimented rule of dressing.

I did get to the stage before leaving Cot Nab of preparing a dinner party with starter as well as main course and proper coffee with obligatory after eight mints! Not forgetting the cheeseboard, always a problem, as Jack liked a mousetrap cheese, and my children, and I were not keen on any cheese.

In a house the size of Cot Nab, before central heating, there was no hostess trolley and other gadgets to make dinner parties easier - the chief trouble was in keeping food hot – especially with the long trot from kitchen to dining room.

Family and close friends round the kitchen table was my idea of entertaining and preferably at mid-day.

We never seemed to have much spare money for clothes, but in York I discovered the first charity shop and I was hooked for life! I've so enjoyed searching (I became very quick to spot one good thing on a long rail) for what I wanted and had some wonderful bargains – even the oddball gown. One of my most loved came from such a shop and would have cost a hundred pounds originally when one thought thirty pounds a lot to pay.

Now in 2005 I'm still a compulsive 'charity' searcher and can hardly pass a shop with out having a quick look round and there are now so many I have to be firm and avoid any glancing in their windows as I walk down the street. Being short and size twelve it's easier to get things my size and even an occasional paid alteration is well worthwhile for a good 'nearly new'.

When we finally left Cot Nab I took many happy memories as well as more sad times, but I did love the view from the kitchen window, the sunsets, playing tennis in summer, and just enjoying the garden with family and friends. I'm inclined to forget long hours of weeding the gravel drive!

Now it was time to uproot again and to move on. When the house in Bishop Wilton was bought, and only weeks left, I found myself thinking 'no big kitchen floor to wash' (I still did it on my hands and knees) 'I'll always have a warm house' or 'there won't be fog down there, and less wind so the garden will be easier'.

All true but thank God for Jack and I being happy together still, to share our joys and our sorrows as we move into semi-retirement with Tony, Pam and their children Mark and Jane leaving their Uncleby cottage for more space at Cot Nab.

Cot Nab

Lill, Mother &'Dotty' leaving Cot Nab - for Garrowby garden party

Garrowby Hall

Jack & Irene with teenage children

Elizabeth Brumfield - Jack & Irene N.F.U. dinner

Tony cleaning tractor 1960's

Jack - snow in the dale, pipe in place!

Tom & Bunky's house, Dinglewood

Irene, Maureen's wedding

Nellie Megginson at a family wedding

*Ken & Joan Voase at
Maureen's wedding*

*Jennifer, Rachel & Maureen,
Cot Nab drive in snow*

*Jack driving
Tom & Jerry,
Irene as groom,
Nostell Priory*

1979. WITTON HOUSE, BISHOP WILTON – LIFE IN A VILLAGE.

The move to Witton House was comparatively easy with an empty, but fully carpeted and curtained house, which could be gradually filled with furniture and other equipment over a few days.

The girls who still lived near helped me to clean it, and to wash paint, but Jack had been busy in the garden over the summer, and it already felt like our home. We even took over the heavy velour curtains in the sitting room and dining room, which lasted throughout our years there.

As soon as our bed was in place, the sitting room furnished and the fire lit, Jack was 'as happy as a sand boy' and really settled in. The T.V. had to be in use too, of course!

I soon had pictures and ornaments in place, and with grandchildren's help, kitchen pots and pans unpacked from boxes. My large collection of books were arranged along the landing until bookcases could be fixed to walls.

Auntie Muriel came to have tea with us on her regular fortnightly visit, and was so surprised to find us so settled. 'It doesn't feel as if you've moved at all'.

I was, at first, very much aware of having neighbours after over forty years of living on what might be called 'isolated farms'. I felt I was being watched every time I went out at the front of the house, and it took time to get used to being part of the village. But I loved being able to walk to see people, to go to the shop, or to church when for years I had relied on being driven and sometimes I used my ancient bike. Neighbours could just 'pop in' and I soon felt happy in the village.

In "A life on the Wolds" I've written of all the work Jack did on the garden and how we got rid of the muddy drive and had a garage built. Jack still went up to work at Cot Nab, but rather at his own choice, other than 'feeding up' each day and helping out regularly with tractor work in busy times and awkward calvings.

I was so pleased not to be at the beck and call of the farm for filling thermos flasks and providing 'lowance!' I still baked quite regularly, but not on the scale of Kingsfield and Cot Nab. I did miss the big kitchen table for baking and the old wooden pastry board. Unit tops leave little room for spreading out bowls and ingredients, though there was much less walking to and fro with fridge in the kitchen and freezer in the utility room.

The central heating was a great joy and even Jack enthused over the extra warmth of the bathroom – 'avocado' suite, very smart, but now of course only white is the 'in' colour.

We even had a bedside telephone, and I thought back to our early married life without any telephone till after we had two babies!

I loved planting out the flower beds, as previous owners just had lawns, and a rockery in the front. Flowers did grow more profusely in a milder climate under the Wolds, and didn't suffer from high winds. Jack took to vegetable production with great zest and we always had fresh vegetables and fruit even up to his last years.

Some of the grand-daughters had ponies in our rented field and Jack improved the former cart sheds we had use of, and made two loose boxes, and places to hang tack. Of course, he had to have driving ponies too, and different vehicles.

Not long into our Witton House years I had the idea of writing to the Dalesman editor Bill Mitchell to see if he would like someone to take over the feature left open after the sudden death of Florence Hopper. Bill replied with 'have you any examples of your work?' So I sent off a few of the N.F.U. Journal contributions, and soon got the request for a date two months ahead. So began twenty five years of monthly articles and the pleasure of readers' letters, and fresh contacts with people I met who liked what I wrote.

Bill asked me to write as if still on the farm so the first few years were called "From a Wolds Farm". I found that part quite easy, but having to write as if three months ahead could be quite difficult. Once when writing my piece, Maureen phoned about ordering coal and I said "Oh it's good to get it now, when its summer". "What do you mean?" she asked because it was springtime and I was thinking in the months ahead.

I gradually got more 'feedback' from the Dalesman articles, and it was encouraging to hear how people enjoyed reading what I had written. Jack seldom showed enthusiasm for my efforts, and I don't think any of the family read them, but Tony would always tell me if he had been asked, "Do you know Irene Megginson?" and seemed pleased to admit he was her son.

I was pleased to be a regular contributor to this popular Yorkshire magazine, and when my friend Joan took me to Clapham when we were having a short holiday nearby, I felt thrilled to meet my editor – dear Bill Mitchell.

Bill made us feel so welcome, on a very wet day, and gave us a tour of the Dalesman premises. I'd always been fascinated by accounts of how the magazine was started in such a small way in the house of the first editor Harry Scott.

Later Jack and I were invited to a lunch in Austwick where we met many interesting and well-known writers. Bill Cowley was the first for a chat, and then Marie Hartley and Joan Ingleby. That was a proud moment – such a famous couple whose writings I'd so enjoyed. When I gave them my name, Marie said, "Oh, we are great admirers" something I shall never forget, and a boost for my ego!

Another 'feather in my cap' was when editor, David Joy, included my article on farm-lads, calling it "To be a farmer's boy" in the hard back book "The Dalesman, a celebration of fifty years". The book was beautifully presented and I even had a friend in London who saw it in Hatchards bookshop, though I don't think he bought a copy!

The second 'lunch' I attended with Bobby Mothersdale after Jack died. Bobby had then joined the magazine as a fellow columnist and we found lots to talk about on the drive through Wharfedale.

That was another happy day, and we had a good photograph taken with dialect expert Arnold Kellett and Terry Fletcher.

I started doing 'talks' too and often Jack would drive me to various venues, often finding someone he could visit in that area, so he could disappear and leave me to it.

Sometimes he would resort to sitting at the back of the hall with a book to read!

My early talks were all of the change of lifestyle from a townie girl to farmer's wife with no 'mod cons' at all and a bit about my writing.

I had always felt I had material at the back of my mind for a book, but never thought about how to get published.

One day I heard through our Vicar that someone wanted to go round our church, St Ediths, to include in a book about Wold churches to be published by Hutton Press. This was in 1985 and it was suggested I show this lady round the church. However, I heard that she – Christine Barker had tried to find me, but as it was the day of Bishop Wilton Show I was on the show field. She did write to me explaining and I think I sent her some church literature. I also (because she had said her mother liked my Dalesman articles) asked if Hutton Press would be interested in a book on my life – mostly as a farm wife. She wrote back saying 'Yes' so I gradually started scribbling on sheets of A4. I wrote at any time often on a board on my knee while sitting in a chair or on the settee with Jack watching T.V. programmes switched on loud!

One winter, it must have been '85 – '86 I did sometimes sit at the dining room table.

When I'd finished the scribbled draft, I carefully copied it all out and let Hutton Press know.

Charles and Dai Brook ran this little publishing company, from their moderately sized private house in Canada Drive, Cherry Burton. "Books of local interest".

Christine was then a director of the company, and I saw more of her when it came to sorting out photographs to include in the book.

I was told there was no need to get my efforts typed as Christine could read my writing and get it onto discs. She lived in Scotland!

We discussed titles and among a few I suggested was 'Mud on my doorstep' which proved very suitable, and easy to remember. Another I thought of was "The unknitted Sock" going back to Mother-in-law thinking I'd be no good as a wife for Jack if I couldn't knit socks! The time involved in getting the book printed lasted many months!

Charles Brook used Clifford Ward printers in Bridlington and he kept saying he'd get it out by Christmas. I even bought a (to me!) expensive checked skirt with tweedy jacket, to wear at the Launch, but I didn't see the printed copies till the day before Driffield Show in July 1987!

Charles appeared with about fifty copies for me to sign ahead, and I had instructions to be at the Hutton Press stand on the showground next morning! There was some publicity in local papers and around Driffield.

The day was rather cold – so I wore a fairly warm dress with matching jacket, not bought new for the occasion – and met a lot of friends and relations while busily signing copies. Charles was pleased, over a hundred I think sold that day.

I had signed a contract beforehand, and was eventually to receive a few hundred pounds royalty fees and the book was reprinted a few times.

The Dalesman reviewed the book, and there was publicity about it in various papers and magazines. I had copies at reduced rates – it was only £3.75 to sell from home, or when giving talks. I even did "Ladies Luncheon Clubs" and charged up to £40, but on those occasions I usually found a friend to drive me who could have a ticket too. I got more confident as a speaker over the years and really enjoyed the meetings, and the talking afterwards to people who often introduced themselves as having known me in earlier days, or had relations who knew me, or others in the Megginson family.

Some surprising connections were quite amazing. When Jennifer drove me to a Conservative afternoon meeting at Scalby near Scarborough, a smart lady came up afterwards and asked "Don't you remember me?" Of course I didn't recognise the blacksmith's daughter from Fraisthorpe! I'd been talking about the village of course, but hadn't said anything detrimental, but may have referred to the work of "Blackie" and we had of course bought a Windsor chair, a bedroom chair and a little pine table with two drawers from his workshop 'junk' and paid ten shillings for the lot!

Evie married a quite successful farmer soon after our wedding, and I was at the time amazed to be asked to attend as a Matron of Honour, which I did at Grindale church wearing one of my honeymoon dresses! Now Evie Stubbins was retired, a widow and living in Scalby – surprise indeed!

While on the book writing years, I followed the first with another "Hutton Press" publication "A little less Mud".

The launch was again at Driffield Show in 1989 on a very hot day – and I remember Sarah looking after little Ian who went to sleep near the tent under the shade of an umbrella. By then Rachel was ill with cancer, and we were so worried about her.

This book also sold well, and again a few hundred pounds to me, but less editions than the first "Mud". I remember well the launch at Sokells Book Shop in Driffield when a constant stream of customers came in for a signed copy. I met all kinds of new and old friends, as well as strangers. One from convent days was Joan Laughton and we have renewed our friendship after not having met since she left school earlier than I did. In 2005 I'd really given up hope of seeing any reprints, in spite of Charles Brook promising them. I've been asked so many times for copies from readers and friends, but Dai Brook died, and I think the Hutton Press has had its day. Small bookshops have closed in many towns and printed matter goes up in price. I still get a small cheque each year from "the public lending right" from books borrowed from libraries!

As I have detailed Rachel's life and early death in my book "Rachel Webb Her Life" I won't repeat all the heartache of those sad years. We published that book privately using the printers in Bridlington who did the Hutton Press books. It sold well and we gave £150 to Cancer Relief.

While on the books still, I wrote a brief history of the convent after it was closed, and this was published by Hutton Press, and sold all the thousand copies. This was in a period of 'Old Girls' Re-unions at Rise Park (before that also closed) and I sold many there as well as it being distributed in shops in the Hull area.

I certainly had more free time at Witton House, and could go to some art classes (which started in Cot Nab years) and still did some china painting.

I enjoyed doing watercolours and found the oils too messy, though one or two still hang on my walls and in friends' houses.

I've told of the mini break holidays in "A Life on the Wolds", but sometimes I would leave Jack and go off on holidays either alone, or with Elizabeth Brumfield, or for shorter ones with Joan who loved to go to the Lake District, or to the Dales where we stay in a B & B with evening meal.

Jack managed on his own with help from family, and neighbours. He was never much good at cooking, but always liked cold meats which were easy, and I'd leave plenty of bacon-cake and pies!

My first flight ever was at the age of seventy when Elizabeth asked me to go with her to Alaska and the Rockies! What a chance!

I found I loved flying and the long flight to Vancouver was uneventful. We had a night there in a luxury hotel and a coach tour of the interesting city around the beautiful estuary where our cruise ship "Sun Princess" was waiting for us. A whole new experience to me and the sail up the Inside Passage was so beautiful, peaceful and quiet. There were only a few British passengers, more from U.S.A. and Germany, but we found kindred spirits in Mel and Olive Davison from Jersey. Our table also had a charming young ship's officer, and a 'difficult' couple from Sussex, the wife always dominating conversations with the wonders of her other travels and family!

There were exciting trips ashore, to the Mernalhall Glacier, Juneau, Ketchican, and Skagway – all unusual towns with lots of interest.

We flew over remote areas of snow-covered mountains and landed with the floatplane on a lake. The thrill of Glacier Bay was unforgettable, also the whale watching evening when we wrapped ourselves in the striped blankets provided and pretended to be Indians – all good light hearted fun, with a lot of laughs with our fellow 'braves' Mel and Olive. We had a good and charming Alaskan girl on the ship most days to give talks on the country and cultures. We also saw salmon in hundreds, some dead, and filling the river completely.

The last morning of the cruise found me seasick with a gentle rolling of the vessel and I had to lie out on deck with a blanket. Elizabeth is a very good sailor.

After the cruise we had an exciting tour of the Canadian Rockies in a coach, still with Mel and Olive. We were very impressed by the mountains, the usual tourist attractions of the snow coach on the Glacier, and the famous hotel at Lake Louise, which was overflowing with big spending parties of Japanese.

I loved the mountain sheep-cum-goats at the top of Banff, and the brilliant blue of lakes. We were lucky to see Mount Robson without cloud, and on our night in Camloops on the way back to Vancouver we met Helen (nee Beaulah) and her husband and family. Helen had lived near Cot Nab when young. I'd also enjoyed two or three swimming pools as the one on Sun Princess was out of use.

My sister Lallie was at that time failing in health while still living in Tunbridge Wells, and I went quite often by train to see her. She also came to York by train and stayed two or three times with us, though becoming slightly confused with Parkinson's disease. Luckily she was met at Kings Cross. It was always a worry meeting her at the station and getting her on at York with her luggage. Once when on a train to Charing Cross from Tunbridge Wells I met an American lady and got talking about hobbies and when I said I did a little writing she was so enthusiastic "I come from 'Gone with the wind' country". I explained I wasn't a novelist, but had an article in "This England" that month. "My favourite magazine, and it will be waiting for me when we get back to Georgia!" So began a friendship with Gaines and Barbara Kimbrough who had a daughter in Farrington married to an English chap.

They visited us at Witton House when in England and once we took them to Rosedale, to stay in "one of your little country pubs"! They were very impressed by the heather in bloom, but exhausted after a morning's walking. Jennifer and William drove to join us on her birthday for dinner and had a happy evening.

I had two holidays on their invitation and flew on my own from Manchester (change at Gatwick) to Atlanta where I was delayed by a storm, so late landing and missed the connection to Sarasota where Gaines and Barbara were on holiday.

It was very exhausting after a very early start that morning to have to phone a Sarasota number to explain – I got a shop assistant to help with the phone and dollars – and found they had already left for the airport! If Jack had been with me, he would have hated it all! There were complications with being offered an earlier flight, but my luggage wasn't transferred as promised and I waited with Barbara and Gaines (who like early bedtime!) till my suitcase eventually arrived, and we could drive to their condo and tumble into bed!

I was thrilled next day to sit on the beach of white sand, to swim in warm clear water with pelicans joining us. Magic!

I only had two days there before they had to head back to Georgia. A long drive, but we stopped on the way at a famous Greek fishing village where real sponges are caught and marketed. I found that place fascinating and bought some little sponges to take home.

I found the American motorways extra ugly and boring – with roadside signs dominating and nothing interesting along the way.

Cumming in Georgia is a small town, and the home of Barbara and Gaines proved to be a bungalow with basement, beside Lake Laneer. Very peaceful and I loved a daily swim in the lake, and a drive all round it with Gaines in his motorboat, in which Barbara had little interest.

I learned a lot about a different lifestyle too, and visited Atlanta with all the "Gone with the Wind" period of history. The big museum set out as an early plantation. I was also taken round a big ornate cinema in the city centre – so popular in the heyday of big American films. Barbara had been there a lot in her youth. It was all styled as a Turkish setting. A guide gave us a tour and we even went on the stage and saw behind the scenes.

Luckily I had no problems on the flight home and Jack, of course, was pleased to have me home. Clothes over there were so cheap; I bought some in the super-market to bring as presents. Jack got pyjamas!

On a second visit, a few years later, Gaines and Barbara were living in "Sun City Centre" on the west side of Florida – when I went for another two week visit.

This was in an 'over 50's' complex – in some ways it didn't seem real! Children only allowed on visits, and all so tidy, similar type one-storey houses, gardens all open plan, and serviced for you – even to watering.

A neighbour had a small swimming pool we were invited to use, and a little 'reception' party was given for me there as a "writer from England".

It was all set out in the lounge, and around the pool, food, drink and conversation. I was asked a lot about life in 'U.K.' and I hope I answered well!

There was a large pool in an entertainment centre where we also went for 'ceramic' classes, used regularly by Barbara who produced some lovely pottery models. I did a small bird on a nest, and bought an alligator for Tony and Pam. There was a jewellery making class as well, and I bought earrings to take home for the girls.

On extra hot afternoons Gaines would retire to bed, and Barbara hired videos like "Driving Miss Daisy". It seemed strange to me to sit in the dark in air-conditioned lounge when the sun was blazing outside.

Twice when cooler in the evenings, Gaines took me in his 'buggy' (a means of getting around used by everyone) to the tennis courts for a game. Quite exhausting as I wasn't used to "singles" by that age.

We did get over to Orlando and Disneyland, and stayed a night in the "Contempary Hotel" where the monorail comes through the lobby. Rather surprised too to find it a usual custom for people to share a large bedroom to save money! I agreed and had one of the two double beds! There was also a single bed and a table and chairs where we ate breakfast we'd taken with us! There was, of course, an en-suite bathroom.

Gaines went to bed early and Barbara and I went down for a late night swim to the pool, which was almost deserted.

I saw quite a lot of Disneyland from the monorail. Barbara showing me the other big hotels – the English one was all set out in British style and served food as in a top class U.K. hotel – even the flowers were all as if picked from an herbaceous border back home. Another was in Mexican style. Later we went to the Epcot centre where I was impressed by the cleanliness and tidiness of everything. The places we went round were so well done, and we felt as if in different countries as it was so realistic.

Very hot there – I've just realised the Epcot experience was the day before leaving to drive back, we saw Sea World and the famous dolphin (Samu?) performing, but no time to see the manatees, which fascinated me.

We visited famous gardens while driving back to Sun City, but didn't find anywhere to eat, other than a posh restaurant, the sort that had a helicopter or private plane landing space. We used the elegant cloakrooms before Gaines decided the food was too expensive!

I bought ice creams in the Gardens, but it was late to eat when we eventually got back to a familiar and reasonably priced restaurant in Sun City!

My half sister Lallie still managed to visit us. She didn't like her small bedroom (compared with the one at Cot Nab) and complained about two beds in it, so we eventually got to the stage of taking one down before she came and propping up the base and mattress along the landing.

In the last year or so of her life, I often visited her in the 'home' in Tunbridge Wells. Sometimes going there and back in a day by train and at other times staying with very kind friends of Lallie, the Plummers, who had a large and lovely home. Also four sons who were at Lallie's school before going on to Ampleforth.

When Lallie died, Jack, Maureen and I went by train for the day of the funeral and the Plummers had a little 'party' afterwards in their house.

Before that Tony drove me down to Tunbridge Wells when Lallie was leaving the home for one with full nursing care, we collected furniture and possessions in the trailer to bring back to store.

I've written so much of Witton House years in my "Jack" book, so won't repeat a lot of it, but Dorothy's visits, my step sister whom I didn't know till Mother re-married at 70 - were happy ones, as she had got over the worst repercussions of her accident and mental illness, she had a great capacity for enjoyment in small things with interest in all the family.

It's funny to look back on, but the picture of Dorothy, which comes to my mind, is of her complete lack of modesty! She was fat, in a "Michelin Tyre" advert sort of figure (younger people will not remember the caricature) and when wanting me to help her to have a morning bath she would waddle along from bedroom to bathroom, quite naked with towel draped over one arm!

Luckily, unlike Lallie she didn't have a long illness, and died soon after enjoying a last Christmas with us in 1986.

Again I went down for the funeral in Bristol by train and stayed over night in the flat, rather than in the 'guest' accommodation as on other visits after she moved to sheltered housing. After the funeral, I met several of her friends I'd known after her accident, and Keith who was executor and her solicitor as well.

I felt I was rather badly done to in some ways as Dorothy had always said all her 'goods and chattels' were for the family, and me and I thought her money too. However it was divided between Keith as well – so not as much as expected. Keith did say "if you have family who need things – please take them" so once more Tony took me with trailer behind to collect bits and pieces of furniture and some 'chattels' including a Royal Worcester dinner service which Dorothy had had as a gift from Lord Attlee's daughter when they worked together at a hospital. It is a large service with lovely tureens and sauceboats and I've since passed it on to Jennifer. We like to think it may have come from the Prime Minister's home!

As, before with Lallie's things we put them out on a bed in the spare room, and let family members choose anything they liked. I can't recall doing anything particular with my small inheritance.

After Lallie died Maureen as her god-daughter inherited what was then quite a large sum, and it did help at a time when Maureen's income was small with which to bring up the three girls "single-handed".

Lallie's son Harvey shared the inheritance, and once told me that he didn't need it, but it would revert back to my family some day! Since then Harvey, for mysterious reasons we can never understand, has cut himself off from all relations, and become a recluse on Vancouver Island. He wouldn't even ask the Fitzpatricks into his house when they called there on holiday, and said "Yes - he did know Rachel had died", but he never wrote to us.

Jack and I had helped him so much in holidays from school when his parents divorced, and always made him welcome on visits from Canada. However "there's nought so queer as folks...."

I managed to still play tennis on the hard courts in the village until over 70 – and Susan English, a good player, would meet me on the court, and we'd make a foursome for doubles.

Country dancing continued, and gave Jack and me great pleasure until old age caught up, and Jack felt unable to "jig around". Those dancing years, weekly classes, and Saturday night visits to other localities for special dances with 'live' bands were great fun with our group of friends.

I was secretary of the W.I. with Lorna Sleightholme as President, and I still continued as Secretary of the Church P.C.C.

We were members of the committee for Cancer Relief, and I acted as Secretary with Angela Cotham.

Angela was Lord Halifax's secretary, and meetings were held at Garrowby Hall, the beautiful new 'mansion' rebuilt by the present Earl on the site of the old inconvenient house – although the chapel, library, and stable courtyard were kept as before.

Lady Halifax was chairman of the committee and we had many fund raising events. For these I had the job of sending out invitations, acknowledging replies and donations, which took up considerable time. We organised such events as 'Pimms Parties', a 'Silent Auction', and an 'Evening Reception' at Garrowby.

Jennifer was also a committee member, during the time she suffered from cervical cancer. We raised a lot of money and helped to start the day unit at Driffield hospital – as well as funding an extra Macmillan Nurse.

I also attended the A.G.M. in London, and went with Lord and Lady Halifax (when they were still living at Givendale) to a meeting in Leeds, and as they were going on to London afterwards, I was chauffeur driven back home!

We continued to have lots of visitors, always enjoyed – and had Lucy and Paul's wedding reception in a marquee on the lawn, but I've described this in my 'Jack' book, and how hard Maureen worked to organise the wedding.

Lucy and Paul lived in Oxford for two years, and I visited them once in their nice little house. They made me very welcome. Before they were married, I stayed a night in the Nurses' home, sleeping in Lucy's bed as she was on night duty!

Lucy was nursing at the Radcliffe then, but in the "Churchill" or was it "Headington" hospital? On one occasion I met up with the mother of my next-door neighbour Jane, as she lived in a nearby village. We were lucky to see part of an episode of Inspector Morse being filmed. We actually saw the famous red Jaguar, and although John Thaw had finished for that day we talked to Kevin Whately, or rather Maria did as more 'forward' than I was!

On one of the visits to Oxford, I met our American friends Gaines and Barbara when they were staying with their family in Faringdon. Anxious to repay some of their hospitality to me, I treated them to lunch at the very grand hotel, "The Randolph" and they were very impressed. I have a photo taken on the beautiful staircase.

Afterwards they were thrilled to go into the grounds of one of the colleges, where students were playing croquet on the lawn in hot sunshine.

Lucy and Paul moved back to York when Paul's job came to an end, and it was when having a meal with them in their nice Edwardian home on York Road that Jack first showed signs of being not quite 'right'. He twice made remarks, which were quite unconnected with the general conversation, and I felt very nervous about being driven home. However, after a good sleep in his chair, and a night in bed, he never knew about what was a type of 'mini-stroke'. Lucy had been sufficiently concerned to phone Tony to make sure we got back safely.

Sadly Lucy and Paul were divorced in 1983 and some time afterwards Lucy decided to go to New Zealand to work, where she was happy for a few years, mostly living in Auckland. Before she left to live "down under" we had a big family party in Witton House, and have a good photograph taken on the stairs.

I've written in detail in the 'Jack' book about his illness, death and funeral so will just say I was thankful he only had a short time as an invalid, a thing he always dreaded. As I write I still think of him constantly, as I do of Rachel, and remember all our good times together.

It wasn't easy to adjust to living without a much loved husband and 'soul mate' after so many years of sharing our lives, but I was fortunate to have family nearby, and also with perhaps the ability to adapt to changes in life.

I was always busy, with dogs Snuff and Daisy to look after, the garden to be responsible for, though 'Howard-next-door' did the lawns and dug the vegetable garden. I paid someone to tackle the hedges, but I coped with all the flowerbeds and there were many little jobs inside and out which Jack had done for me, though never domesticated in the way many husbands are today.

A small compensation was to become 'boss of the telly' as one thing we didn't share always was enjoyment of all programmes. Many times I would have switched off, but Jack liked the sound of the T.V. and always louder than I needed it. Even if he was dozing in his chair, and I would sneak across the room (before 'remote control') he would wake up with a start "what have you switched that off for?"

I just had to 'switch off' myself to carry on writing, or reading, and was perhaps lucky to be able to do this.

Rachel's widower, Norman was not well at the time of the funeral, and having trouble with what he thought of as indigestion. He gradually became ill with hospital investigations, and it was a difficult time for us, who tried to help with him and Ian.

Maureen had planned to visit Lucy in February 1999, so she suggested I join her. I was excited by the thought, and in due course flights were booked. Lucy made great preparations for a tour of both islands, and was taking three weeks off work, and arranged for a nursing friend Jill to visit at the same time so we could travel around together.

Sadly Norman's health had deteriorated, and he looked so thin and poorly. Poor Ian at 12 was going to Longcroft School in Beverley, and had to learn to live with illness in the house. People were very good about helping, other than our family, local friends and especially the Marshals as Robert and Ian were great pals. Shirley still helped in the house and Jason outside of course. Norman was admitted to hospital in Beverley before Maureen and I set off on our holiday in New Zealand, so we kept in touch by phone while having that wonderful sight-seeing tour and meeting Lucy's friends too who were sharing a house in Auckland.

I kept a diary of the three weeks, and on return made a scrapbook with photos, and illustrations of places we visited. Lucy was a first class organiser, and booked accommodation ahead for each night of our two week tour. Mostly very inexpensive 'chalet' type places – sometimes with a bathroom, and good sleeping space. Always a cooker, but sometimes we had to use loos and showers across the lawns of the complex. One night on the phone I heard Lucy say "could you give us a chalet near the shower block as I have my grandmother with me".

For more details of this memorable holiday, you must consult the diary I kept. I was there for my birthday and the girls took me out for a meal at a restaurant under Mount Cook, which was most enjoyable. We 'dressed up' for the occasion as usually one or other (never me – though I'd set a table and wash up) cooked the evening meal wherever we were sleeping that night.

In Christchurch we were at a Youth Hostel, so Maureen cooked in the communal kitchen and we ate at a table there. We could use a washing machine too, which was a luxury.

We learned one night that Norman had died, and that Pam was the last of the family to visit him in hospital and we thought of poor Ian.

There were many highlights, and much fun in New Zealand. I'll always remember the swim in the lake at Waneka after the Horse Show there and watching the wee penguins at dusk returning to their babies after a difficult climb up a rocky slope.

The final night's lodging on the road was much the worst place, with no blame on Lucy, but it turned out to be more of a schoolboys' holiday camp! No cooking facilities so they went out for a takeaway; not my choice! The lads were noisily enjoying themselves around the hall.

The beds were institutional in sparse cabins and Mo and I felt we couldn't use the pillows without covering them with our own garments first. I remember sitting on the iron-framed bed, looking across at Mo, and saying, "I don't think this would suit Lorna and Sybil" who were village friends who liked 'posh' hotels!

We had two nights again in Auckland before saying a sad goodbye to Lucy and flying back home. We were met at York station by Sarah who drove us to Bishop Wilton and gave us a dramatic account of the worry they'd all gone through, especially Geoff and Jennifer, as Rebecca had given birth to a premature baby Sophie, only two pounds or so in weight. However, Sophie had not been the real concern, as it was Becca who developed a very serious condition involving her kidneys among other complications. She was in Hull Infirmary and the baby in Hedon Road Maternity Hospital. All had expert care, but it had been a horrendous time with Becca unable to wee, and Sophie being brought to her in an incubator to look at. We were so sad to hear all this, but relieved that the crisis was over, and all progressing well. Jennifer had gone to a lot of trouble to keep all this disturbing news from us while on holiday, but she had also had the additional worry of Norman's death and funeral with young Ian on her mind too.

Ian was cared for at Cot Nab, and took over what had been Mark's bedroom with all his parents' furniture, his farmyard and childhood treasures, after some time with the Marshall family.

The next difficult task was having to empty Bygot House; Norman hadn't left an up-to-date will, which made everything more problematic. The executors were not popular, but there was no option but to have meetings and discussions. Tony was official guardian and he was under the regulations of local authorities.

All the family helped with the mammoth task of sorting out Norman and

Rachel's possessions, emptying drawers and wardrobes where nothing had changed since Rachel's death. Homes and storage space had to be found for furniture and many articles, books, to save, and bin bags of unwanted stuff for disposal or charity shops.

I'll always remember twelve year old Ian being present when we were deciding about the pine furniture – and Ian said to Mark who was shortly to marry Kate "I'll give the table and chairs to you and it will be the best present you'll get!"

There were heart breaking decisions and agonising memories, but after a few weeks the house was empty. Jason helped with Norman's friends to see to the outside stock (live and dead) and to arrange a sale.

Financially Norman just could not have carried on farming in the way he did. It was all very sad, but eventually the house and buildings were let, and the land let to some of the Cook family. This proved good for Ian over the following years.

Ian settled to school in Pocklington at Woldgate, with no great interest in academic subjects, but he found a friend from a farming background in Colwyn Stonehouse, and they shared many activities together out of school.

William helped a lot by taking Ian to the Gun Club near Bygot, as he showed talent, and did well with the 'clays'.

Whenever there was a chance to go 'beating' for William's shoot, or at Garrowby, or shooting rabbits in the dale, Ian would be there full of enthusiasm. Tony and Pam cared for him well.

Mark and Kate were married in quite a lavish style, and we all enjoyed the day in glorious weather near Selby. Ian was in his element as an usher complete with morning suit and top hat.

Pam had done wonderful dressmaking with her own 'Bridegroom's Mum' outfit and Jane's bridesmaid's dress.

I had been to stay with Tom and Bunky in the previous summer, and Bunky seemed well, except for complaining about a pain in her side. However, she often had back trouble over the years, so I wasn't unduly worried. In the autumn she wrote to say she had been diagnosed with gall bladder trouble and was to have an operation.

I phoned Tom the weekend of the operation and was devastated to learn that they had been unable to operate as they found a large cancer of the liver. Another life long friend going out of my life! I felt so sad to think I wouldn't see Bunky again. Such a lively personality and memories crowded my thoughts. We had had much fun together even after she left Hull to live in Braintree, aged eleven, we still visited each other in summer holidays, and wrote long letters after our marriages.

At least we had to find comfort in the fact that she hadn't known a long illness, and was never conscious after the operation.

Tom was very strong in his great loss, and before the funeral asked if I would give a tribute to Betty as I had known her longer than anyone. I felt this would be a difficult but important task, and agreed to do it as I hoped it would help all the family.

Tony, Pam, Jennifer and I went to Gawsworth for the funeral, and I managed to give the Eulogy by looking beyond the family to the back of the church.

People were so kind about what I had said and asked for copies to keep – now no one left to call her Bunky.

As at all funeral gatherings, there was joy in meeting up with family and friends, and we all gathered at the bungalow in Fytton Close before we set off for the long journey home.

That was still in the same year as Jack's death, so I have got out of sequence in putting it in the following year!

I am not referring to diaries in these memories, so readers must forgive such mistakes.

In 1999 I celebrated my 80th birthday with a lunch party for mostly family at Cot Nab. I remember making an apple dumpling steamed pudding to add to the meal provided by family, as it had been such a favourite in Tony's young days.

I had a lot of extra jobs to do after Jack's death, in trying to keep house and garden in good shape.

Jack had always carried in coal and logs, and like lighting fires, if not cleaning up the hearth in the mornings!

While on my own, I had smaller fires and less mess than the 'piled up the chimney' type, so loved by Jack. I also sat in his chair, or my smaller one near the fire with the dogs.

In April 1999 Tony, Pam, Ian and I had a day flight to Iceland and thoroughly enjoyed it all.

It was Ian's first flight and he was so thrilled to be in the air and having a meal brought on the way, before we landed outside Reykjavik

We were taken on a tour by bus, stopping to see things of special interest. I was quite amazed by the huge municipal swimming pool, where swimmers were gaily going to and fro outside in April!

The houses all had brightly painted tin roofs and I liked walking along a quay where whaling boats were lying redundant, and snow-capped mountains made a background to the town.

The moonlike ground cover seemed strange when we were driven in open countryside, stopping at a lovely simple little church, but the so-called highlight was the Blue Lagoon.

It all sounded so romantic, but the surroundings were more like a power station in a very bleak area!

Tony opted out of swimming, but Pam, Ian and I went into bare and comfortless sheds to change. The brief scurry to the pool was freezingly cold, but once in the water one felt marvellous. We hardly needed to swim as so buoyant, and Ian was thrilled, and said, "If I lived here, I'd come every day".

The journey home was uneventful, and though we'd been given an hour or two in the shops of Reykjavik, we had few parcels, as the prices were sky high.

A day to remember and we felt we'd like to go again and see more of the countryside.

In the Millennium New Year I had a bad chest infection, which started on Boxing Day, and Jennifer rushed me off to the doctor for antibiotics. The infection took some time to shake off, and I wasn't well, when Ian came to spend the night of this momentous New Year with me. There were celebrations in the village and bells to be rung. Ian said he would go down to see what was happening, but fell asleep on the settee, and I was ready for bed, so neither of us joined in any celebration to welcome the 21st century!

I mustn't forget to record a most wonderful Millennium experience in going with Elizabeth Brumfield to Oberammagau for the passion play.

I have kept a journal of all that memorable holiday – as of other holidays if anyone reading this is interested.

As well as The Play – quite a day of being intensely absorbed by the whole stupendous performance – we were with a coach tour organised by Cottingham Church group – and we toured not only Austria, but also Switzerland and France. Even a day in Italy – we saw a great deal of Europe in a short time – and even fitted in Communion services daily!

Earlier before Jack died (I think it was!) Lorna and I joined a W.I. trip for a week in the Loire valley. That was a happy experience, good company and rather mediocre hotel! I shared a room with a lady called Gina – ex matron and quite a character. She was even older than I and died the following year. North Sea Ferries – oh yes I'm sure Jack met us off the coach in Driffield.

Lorna was still lame after fracturing her hip in a simple fall.

I think it was also in the year 2000 that Anne Bendall came to stay a few days in April, and it was lovely to see her again. Another visitor was Mickey and while she was here we were joined by Dick (nee Hewitt) now Haffland from California. Dick had known Mickey better than I in convent days, as their mothers were friends, but we had met at a reunion and kept in touch after that. Dick was only with us for two nights, after being met at York Station, but we had a lot of fun, as she was still exuberant as in school days, and we had much laughter and met up with my family. Pam kindly drove us to Malton where Dick was handed over to Margaret Squire, another friend of convent days, and was driven off to Wass near Byland in a smart open sports car! Mickey stayed on for a little longer. In those days she could still manage the rather complicated train journey back to Northants.

Coidy, who we first knew as one of the Hyde girls at Fraisthorpe, was with us again as a lively guest though approaching her 90th birthday – and while with us we had a lovely lunch party when Margaret and Max Clarkson visited from Newark.

Margaret had illustrated the hardback copy of Coidy's "Life in a Liberty Bodice" with her wonderful pictures. I had been in touch with Margaret some years before through an article in the Yorkshire Post magazine about her 'nostalgia' paintings and later was invited to meet her when giving an exhibition at the Theatre Royal in York after making a series of the pantomime artists with Berwick Keiller.

I was fascinated by her pictures and ordered a signed copy of "Cleaning the Cupboards" and gave Pam one as a birthday present, so, I really think Coidy met Margaret and Max through me, and she stayed with them when deciding on the book illustrations.

Jennifer cooked a very good pheasant casserole as part of our lunch menu – they were so homely and such an easy couple to entertain.

In 2002 my book "A life on the Wolds" was published with the help of Winston Halstead, "The Yorkshire Ridings" magazine editor who made Jennifer and me very welcome – also his small staff of two in the small offices up a steep flight of stairs in a building at the end of his garden in Driffield.

We had a very successful book launch after taking delivery of 1500 copies from printers in Wiltshire. I began to wonder how and where I could store them all and if ever they would be sold!

The launch was in early December with an 'open' day at Witton House. The family acted as hostesses throughout the day with grand-daughters also helping. We provided refreshments and many people came. I was kept busy signing copies and it was a good start.

We put a notice in the Dalesman and I posted about 60 copies through that. We supplied Sokells in Driffield, Forths in Pocklington, and Hoppers in Malton, also Beverley Book Shop. I also got some delivered to Browns in Hull and a few to Waterstones, but dealing with large multiple firms is rather involved.

Over the next two years they sold well, and with encouragement from Jennifer I ordered another 800 copies.

Now in 2005 I have 3 left, and I made a good profit much to my amazement. Of course there were the ever-welcome letters from readers.

Around this time more houses were added to Hall Garth where our stables had been in our pony days.

We had been friendly with Norman and Hilary Haines before Jack died, but they left Hall Garth to live near Liverpool. Barbara Caines came to live in one of the bungalows, and Jill and Digby Machin built a big house nearer the paddock, with another going up near them, and six or eight small houses on the roadside rather blocking views from the original bungalows.

Before this new century, both Alison and Sarah, Maureen's daughters, were living in York. Alison with Duncan, and Sarah alone in Amber Street, which she bought in a rather run down state, but soon, made it a pleasant little house.

Alison became a qualified nursery nurse and Sarah struggled valiantly with accountancy exams while working full time for Costcutter. She also joined the Territorials, so had a lot to fit in, and for a time had Neil living in at Amber Street, meeting through the Territorials.

Maureen had been working for some years as Susan Webster's chief carer. Susan had been badly injured in a car accident soon after her marriage to Dr. Webster, and as a result needed full time care.

After a long period of devoted attendance to Susan, Dr. Webster wished to re-marry – and Susan eventually was moved to York where her Mother supervised round-the-clock care.

Maureen did not want to become part of that team, so looked for another job, we were all glad that by that time Maureen had a happy relationship with Barry Lonsdale – and they divided their lives between his house in Pocklington and her cottage in Bishop Wilton.

Luckily Maureen also found a job to suit her personality as receptionist at "Take it Easy" in Pocklington.

In January 1999 we had another big family event – the wedding of Jane to 'Curly' otherwise Richard Cartledge!

Curly was one of Mark's friends, and also part of the group with Michael

Stringer and Warren Dykes. He was an only child, and lived in Bolton with his parents John and Sue.

January 16th was a bright, cold and frosty day, with a hint of snow earlier on.

Kirby Underdale church looked lovely in the sunlight and Jane made a beautiful bride.

Pam (of course) had made the very elegant bridal gown in a goldy fabric, over which she wore a little navy velvet jacket.

The bridegroom and groomsmen had dark green morning suits. No bridesmaids.

After the church service we went up to Cot Nab where the 'tatie-store' had been transformed with a huge marquee erected within the walls! Not only that but also luxury toilet area and a kitchen for the 'Simply Delicious' caterers. One setback was an electric fault, which caused some delay and rather cold surroundings for the first part of the reception, but groomsman Warren (electrician) soon put it right.

A very good meal followed and dancing went on into the late evening. I came home in between to see to Daisy and to have a rest. It was also Curly's birthday so more celebrations.

The "happy couple" had bought a little bungalow in Fangfoss and made it very attractive. I remember Ian being very interested, but thought there should be a spare bedroom in case he wanted to stay!

Curly was a "panel-beater" with a firm on Sutton Business Park and his hobby was car racing in which his father John was also interested. Jane was working at the new big MAAF organisation near Stamford Bridge.

So for a time Pam and Tony were on their own at Cot Nab except for Ian who helped round the farm and still showing little interest in school work.

My life at Witton House continued much as usual and there was the sad death of Enid Sykes. Enid the wife of Jack's cousin on his mother's side had been failing in health, both physically and mentally for some years, with Beilby showing devotion and patience.

Derrick Sykes, known as Bill to many, would call for me to visit Beilby and Enid, and sometimes his sister-in-law went to. They kept their large and pleasant bungalow rather low in temperature, with the result in winter of many complaints on the way home, of how frozen we'd all been! It had been the same before they moved from the farm at Tibthorpe, as even colder there!

Enid died in hospital, and Derrick took me to the funeral. After that Beilby seemed determined to go out and about more, making up for several restricted years. I had some happy days out with him and sometimes with others joining us. One day, with Freda Watts we went up to the moors and had a lovely picnic, which Beilby had prepared.

However, sadly, Beilby became ill with a form of leukaemia. Derrick and I visited him in Bridlington hospital twice, and when quite frail he called on me at Witton House, wearing slippers and carrying his beloved old Dachshound in his arms.

Lucy was living with me for a few months, and she was home that afternoon, so brought in a tray of tea.

Lucy was buying a little modern house in Pocklington, and working as a nurse at the Malton Bacon factory. She was very welcome to stay with me till her house purchase was completed, and I enjoyed the company, also tales of the trials and tribulations of life in the factory.

When Beilby died, Derrick took me again to the funeral at Kirkburn Church, and afterwards we met up with many people at the farmhouse where Mark Sykes was then living, and running the farm.

So ended association with the Sykes family at Tibthorpe and I thought back to a visit as far back as our engagement time, and being invited to what we called a "hot tea", probably pheasant or guinea fowl.

We used to see quite a lot of Uncle Fred and Auntie Flo in following years.

Now Derrick at Poppleton was the only one left of that family. Mark was an adopted son and as far as I know hasn't married, or taken a partner.

My westie Daisy was a companion to me all the remaining years at Witton House, but Snuff, Jack's dear little crossbred terrier suffered from fits in old age, and I was grateful to Jennifer when further deterioration meant the end was near, and Jen kindly took her to the vet.

I missed Snuff very much, but Daisy seemed unaffected by the loss of a companion she'd known all her life.

I have many memories of Witton House years – of visitors – ponies, grandchildren, and 'greats' – many changes, but we still kept up the family picnics at Levisham each summer with more people as the gathering increased.

Ian kept up the vegetable garden and made a much better job of it than revising for school exams! Biking up the hill after gardening was the hard part.

Our rector James had a back operation and was unable to toll the church bell when the Queen Mother died, so I felt quite honoured to do it by slowly ringing while paying tribute to a very great and much loved lady with one hundred and one tolls.

Another time when Prince Charles was a guest at Garrowby he came to St. Edith's with Lord Halifax and I read the lesson only a yard from His Royal Highness. I thought it was so nice for him to attend a service with no fuss (even if extra congregation arrived) and when they left there were no people around the village or near the church gates.

I was beginning to feel that looking after Witton House and with the high ceilings – lots of paintwork, and much needing doing in the way of decorations and improvements it was getting too much to cope with.

Thus, I wasn't really worried when Tony said he'd found a house he and Pam would like to buy! Mark's marriage, which had seemed so happy, had sadly ended in separation, with the Fridaythorpe house sold and Mark back at Cot Nab.

I had naturally expected that when I left Witton House, that Tony and Pam would live in it, but I soon realised they would prefer to sell it, and to find somewhere of their choice, rather than 'follow on' as they had had to at Cot Nab.

So – like Jack when Tony suggested we should move out of Cot Nab, I gave the stipulation "I don't want to live anywhere other than Bishop Wilton!"

The Witton House years will always be memorable for the family gatherings, big parties, lots of visitors, callers and also for my writing years when three books were published by Hutton Press. Then followed "Rachel Webb" and "A life on the Wolds" with, of course, the regular "Dalesman" column that gave much in the way of 'feedback' correspondence. The talks especially "Farm lads of the East Riding" continued to be popular and through them I met people with interesting connections while buying my books.

In the years before I left Witton House I had a long awaited visit from the "Dalesman" editor Terry Fletcher. I had asked all three editors during my time with the magazine to call on me if in the area, but none of them made it, though I had met them in Clapham, at special lunches and also Jack and I called on Terry in the new offices in Broughton Hall. So – I was thrilled one morning when Terry phoned to say he was coming to York and could call in the morning. I said that would be fine, but my grand-daughter Rebecca was coming to lunch with her little girl Sophie.

Terry hadn't time to stay long, but I made him welcome – he'd never been to the village – and gave him coffee and crunch or whatever was in the tin!

We talked generally, and Rebecca arrived with Sophie – so more conversation before Terry said he must go to the next appointment.

With Rebecca and Sophie staying on, we had lunch before going to Pocklington and Burnby Gardens where Sophie liked the fishponds, and the adventure playground.

That evening Terry phoned to say he hadn't had the chance to tell me that they were changing the format of "Dalesman" in some ways, and would not include my "Wolds Village" after the next month, but as you've already sent in the month following we will pay for that!!!

Some shock, and I still feel it was rather an underhand way to dismiss me after about twenty five years! No doubt, I was getting to be 'passed they sell by date" but I got little in the way of thanks.

I asked if I could add a paragraph to my last column to say how sorry I was that my association with the magazine must end, but that was not allowed as they were making the decision! So they added the news that I was retiring!

The chief compensation was in receiving many letters from readers, which I have kept – all saying 'thank you' and some refusing to continue subscribing!

I thought the magazine could afford to keep sending a free copy each month, but no such luck – and when a village friend died, I no longer saw it as he had passed it on to Eileen Hopper who passed it on to me! So now I never see it!

I did write one of my "odd odes" about it all and sent Terry a copy. I don't really resent the termination, only the way it was done! I've nothing but good memories of the years of being a contributor.

Before leaving the "Witton House" years, I mustn't forget to mention the sad loss of Phyllis Sturrock a village friend, and the fact that after Jack's death when Phyllis became an invalid, I became a caller most mornings on my way to the shop.

Phyllis had 'carers' coming in, but there was a gap before the night sitter was replaced by a day time carer – so I took to being there when she got up, and into dressing gown while I made her breakfast porridge!

Phyllis did wonderful tapestry pictures and in her final year still produced ones of flowers. Three of which – nicely framed she gave us as thank you presents to Susan English, Lorna Sleightholme and me! I was so pleased with mine, I think I had first choice, and it hangs in my hall now.

Phyllis's house was full of good antiques, china and books and after her death it was sad to find out that beloved god-children, so often talked about by Phyllis who lacked close family, soon had the house emptied with a large furniture van from Tennants Antiques of Bedale on the doorstep!

I did choose a watercolour of the village when friends other than the godchildren were in the house and offered me a gift.   An entertaining personality, a spinster school mistress, a good friend and I hope she never knew how little her valuable treasures were appreciated, apart from the money value!

Another sadness was when David English became ill after a serious stroke.

Jennifer and William who lived next-door had become almost as good friends of the English's, as I was – they, the English's, would often ring and ask me to go round for a cup of tea and in winter to sit over their fire for a chat – especially so, after Jack died.

I was able to see David in hospital, and on my last visit I felt I'd said a final 'goodbye', and so it was as he died soon after that.

Susan was very brave and her family helped her a lot.   She continued to help me to clean the brass eagle in church, and we often met together. She made one or two improvements in the house to make life easier, and she had the car to drive around and to go visiting.   So – it was another blow when Jennifer and William discovered she had had a stroke.   The family were told, and her son in Beverley came quickly as she was in hospital for some time.   Daughter Jane came up from Reading to help, and to visit, but it was a shock to find the very active Susan reduced to little movement, and at first little conversation.

However, eventually we were visiting Susan in a 'home' at Dunnington which proved to be depressing, with little stimulation for a stroke patient.

Susan improved so much, and was able to go out in a car, or in a wheel chair.   One day I gave a lunch party for her with village friends, and her old friend Joan Atkinson coming to join us from Garton.   Susan came by "wheelchair taxi" and it was lovely for her, and for us, to have the meal together.

Now Susan is in a very pleasant 'home' in Bielby and we visit when we can.   She still keeps up her interest in T.V. Sport and in reading 'Horse and Hound', but can't walk unaided, or to use her right hand.

Lots of times David and Susan joined Jack on pony drives, and were always ready to take part in village fund-raising activities.

Now in the summer of 2002, I was ready to pack up what I wanted and to move down the village!

Tony said the only house available just then was a rented end of terrace cottage near Jennifer – so we (Tony, Jennifer and I) went to look round with the agent in July.

As soon as I walked through the hall to the kitchen I said, "This will do!" I felt it was all I needed a small house to be, as we explored more. I liked the tiled floor (red) of the kitchen-cum-dining room, the turquoise painted units, the Aga and the fact that there would be room for my precious old sideboard bought with old 'Dotty's compensation money!

Further inspection showed a secluded little courtyard, a back porch, small sitting room with 'old-style' fireplace, three bedrooms and bathroom. I would have liked a downstairs loo, but no room for one.

So we decided to apply for the tenancy, £495 a month, and soon heard that I had been accepted as a tenant by Jenny Debenham who had 'bought to let'.

After that there were many setbacks and disappointments for Tony and Pam.

They expected to put Witton House on the market for a quick sale, but first they heard they couldn't sell without living there themselves for six months. So there were many frustrating delays.

But – the dye was cast as the saying goes, and with a lot of family help, I packed up all necessary for my move to the little cottage by the beck, and in August I moved, leaving many, many, happy memories of Witton House years.

Before starting on "Corner Cottage" years, I have looked up a few diaries, which I'd thought I could do without!

Then I kept asking myself "Did that happen before or after I moved?" and I find I am left with events to include in the 'Before' years.

One was, Jennifer's step daughter, Katy Foster's wedding to Jon Shepherd – another happy wedding day in April 2000, also like Jane's, at Kirby Underdale Church.

Kate wore a beautiful dress, and with pretty bridesmaids in blue (I specially remember Elizabeth Foster) it was all very pleasant in, and around the churchyard for photographs.

The reception was in a marquee at Forest Farm, and I sat at the same table as William's parents, Charlie and Mary. Charlie, then ninety four, had lent his Jaguar for the bride and groom!

There was a good meal, and during the disco (noisy as usual) we could go into the more peaceful surroundings in the house if we wished.

Before leaving the dance floor I did win a bottle of something(?) for taking part in an action number!

Colin Newlove's daughter, Lyn, was in the house as a nanny (her profession) for the group of young children, and after talking to her I realised she was to be married the following week. Colin quite famous as an animal trainer in my other books, often talked to me on the phone after Jack died. Colin phoned the next day to say Lyn would like me to be a guest at her wedding, and they could arrange transport to Thornton-le-Dale church if I would like to go. So another lovely wedding day and I didn't mind going alone as so many people I knew. At the reception at "The Forest and Vale" Pickering we could sit out on the garden terrace in warm sun, and at the meal I was with people who had known Rachel, in particular the Warrens at whose home Colin and Helen were married in Buckinghamshire and where Rachel had spent time in her eventing years.

Pam kindly drove over to Pickering to collect me at the end of the celebrations, and I did appreciate my late invitation.

After Jack died, I saw more of Joan who featured a lot in my other books. She would often drive over, and we would go out shopping, or for picnics.

Once we went all the way to Ulverston to see an elderly relative of Joan's – a sweet old lady of ninety who lived alone. She wouldn't come out for a drive, but we took meals to her, while staying near Coniston water.

Another time we stayed in a small hotel I'd been to with Jack and our walking group, and on two other short little holidays we found B & B's (with evening meal) in houses in the Dales. We visited one Dalesman reader in West Witton one evening, who sent me regular Christmas cards, even when living in Hong Kong. We met his charming Chinese wife too, and had a very interesting visit.

By 2000 Joan was quite ill, after heart troubles and spells in hospital. One 'diary' entry says "Joan came, the first time she'd driven as far as this since being ill".

In that December, Nancie, Elizabeth and I took part in the school Christmas entertainment in the village hall. Good fun and we were so well received we were asked to join in another year in the church.

I also went to Bobbie Mothersdales to meet Harry Gration for a BBC recording (radio) to be heard on Boxing Day morning. Sue Ellis the BBC lady was so nice she drove me to and fro, and stayed for a good lunch in the Mothersdale kitchen. Harry was charming but had to rush off to another job. None of us heard the radio programme, but a friend in the south caught it on car radio! I did get a copy from BBC.

My sister Olive was failing in health after her 90th birthday. I often had her over to Witton House with Suzanne.

Olive who had been so active and healthy had about two years of failing mind, as well as body. Suzanne her youngest and the only family member near enough had a hard time with regular visits to her mother.

I sometimes went to the Pocklington bungalow, but it was easier for Suzanne to take Olive to Witton House. Conversation became difficult and Olive was very reluctant to have carers calling, also she was not co-operative with the medical people.

Also in 2001, I went with Elizabeth on a canal "Hotel Barge" holiday. We had a lovely week with pleasant friends and crew, all ending in Bath and Bristol. We had two nights with Elizabeth's "Nutter" friends near Dorchester to end with, but travel was difficult with suitcases and trains not connecting.

We came back by 2 coaches on a very hot day, which was a rather frustrating end to our lovely canal week. Later in the following year we had another peaceful canal holiday, but an excellent driver to and from destinations in Elizabeth's car. Luxury indeed.

I really made up my mind at last to go to Switzerland as Adrienne kept saying 'come' also Nora Loftus Bryan who had retired there, so I flew off from Manchester (train there) and was met in Geneva airport by Adrienne, Peter and son David. It was wonderful to see their lovely home again above the lake. Last time there, was on our European tour with the Fitzpatricks!

Adrienne and I had a wonderful day across the lake in the small French town Yvoir and I had a very relaxing few days with some of their family who were living in the lower flat for school holidays.

Nora who had been a good friend in Bishop Wilton gave me another few days of friendship, exploring the very interesting and historic city. I had B & B at a small hotel - English spoken! - and we had a day going by coach along the lake to a lovely little village, and tea in Marie Clare's amazing house and lakeside garden. No trouble with flights and I came back filled with the joy of old friends and lovely Switzerland.

In that last year at Witton House we had the sad news in February of Pam Layzell's death.

It was a great loss to me, though I knew she was ill in hospital, and had talked to Roy on the phone.

Pam and Roy had been a close couple, who did everything together, and I wondered how Roy would cope, but like Tom Sloan he was amazingly strong. I thought, of course, of all the years Pam and I had been so close, especially in Park Avenue years.

We walked to school together, had a similar sense of humour, played board games, cards and practised standing on our heads or hands. Lots of outings together with Mother driving us, and those unforgettable Lakeland holidays. Pam's mother and sisters in Hull, growing up and seeing less of each other, but the bond of childhood saw us through to adult life, and keeping in touch with long letters. Visiting each other after marriage and getting to know both lots of families.

Tony took Jennifer and me to the funeral in Woodhall Spa, and again I had been asked to pay tribute to Pam in the service in the Catholic church.

We went to the Hoyes farm first, to meet all the family, before going to church. It was all rather informal, with the very Irish Priest chatting to the small congregation, and to us like old friends. He was told I was to speak and I stood near the coffin, when I'd finished, he and others applauded, to my surprise. At least the service was different and he also said I could go and help him out any time!

The family asked for the eulogy to have copies made as Tom's family did.

It was lovely to spend time at the farm with Pam and Roy's large family, of all ages, but coming home I felt very much the loss once more of a dear old friend.

A month after Pam Layzell's death my half-sister Olive died in York hospital. Olive had not been in hospital long, and I only visited her once when she hardly knew I was there.

Her son Malcolm from Bournemouth and daughter Shirley from Jersey arrived to stay in the Pocklington bungalow and after the death they cleared it out ready to hand back to the relatives of Olive's second husband.

There was an incredible amount of clothes, but also a great collection of biscuits, sweets and chocolates of all kinds, unopened in boxes or tins! Olive's family didn't want any, so I took the lot! Even 'past sell by date' were in perfectly good condition, so were passed on to my family and village friends, or to be used as raffle prizes (if within sell by date) and were appreciated.

Various other so called 'junk' I took to be sold at 'bric a brac' stalls and after the small funeral at Hull Crematorium we went to the bungalow for the last time.

I felt Suzanne deserved more than anyone for the care she had given to a Mother who was not exactly a devoted, loving type, although Olive had great pleasure in visiting Shirley in Jersey for many holidays.

As a 'sister' to me, we had never found a great deal in common, but we 'got on' in a rather remote fashion, and I was relieved that at 91 she had had a short time in hospital – and lived independently in her own home, only giving up her chief pleasure of cards and coach trips for a comparatively short time. In middle age Olive had been a very good bowler and played for the county in many matches up and down the country.

Tony and Pam now had a grand-daughter, Laura Grace, born to Jane and Curly. They had moved from their small bungalow to a Victorian house on the main street in Bolton, which belonged to Curly's parents, but thinking ahead, they had converted a barn across the yard into a very pleasant home, so the two families lived close together and shared a big garden. Luckily they all got on well together, and Susan and John also delighted to have a grandchild whose birthday was February 14th.

A lot happened in that month – apart from the deaths of Pam and of Olive, Joan was ill again and in hospital.

The most tragic time was in early February when William's daughter Katy had a baby, Cameron who was born with a gap in his oesophagus, and rushed off to Newcastle Hospital while Kate recovered from a caesarean operation.

There followed five weeks of intense worry for all the family. Wee Cameron had a series of operations, as he also had a heart defect, and Kate with Jon became residents at the hospital (two different hospitals dealt with the operations) and for a time Jennifer and William took the caravan up to a park near Newcastle to give support to Jon and Katy.

Cameron must have been a tough baby, and perhaps many prayers helped, but he did pull through. There have been setbacks, but now he is a sweet little lively three year old.

I went to Wales in April and had lunch with Tom Sloan after being met by the Fitz's at Chester.

Bishop Wilton Show, and the usual summer activities in the village – but now I had to do the final packing up at Witton House. On August 9th it was moving day – damp and drizzly, but more helpers than expected – perhaps due to it being poor harvest weather.

Witton House from garden

Witton House, Bishop Wilton

Bishop Wilton, Cloudburst Sunday

*Irene bell ringing for a wedding,
St. Edith's Church*

Tony & Pam in sitting room - once the kitchen

Ian at Bygot, aged three

First book signing, Driffield Show

Barbara and Gaines visit and walk in Rosedale with Irene

Mickey and 'Oxo' relax in sitting room

Irene and Sally with Ian, Christopher & Nicola at Flamborough

Ian with Sarah, Christopher and Nicola at Bygot after Radel died

Four Mrs Megginson's - Doreen, Pam, Irene and Janet, Witton House garden after lunch party

Megginson lunch party after Jack had died. All 'Megginson' except Maureen Metcalfe (3rd from right) & Jennifer Foster (near left)

'Life on Wolds' launch with Sally, Rebecca, Nicola & Sophie

Witton House launch of book about Jack. Irene, Jennifer & Maureen with Lucy, Sarah & Alison

Irene and Maureen on Mount Cook, New Zealand - 1998

2002. LIFE IN CORNER COTTAGE.

So, after much re-reading of diaries, I hope I've forgotten nothing I should have recorded in the final period of Witton House.

I knew I'd miss the beautiful hall and staircase, the views, the much-loved garden, but I was really glad to stop working so hard and picking rasps so continuously!

In Corner Cottage it was lucky that the carpets were all down and nothing I could disapprove of. Also I loved all the bright colours chosen by the last owners – just flat white paint for woodwork, but emulsion in blues, yellows and pale greens for the walls.

Only my bedroom was too deep a shade of violet, and I changed that after some time to a more delicate heather. The vast fitted cupboard in my bedroom was a lifesaver for a lot of beloved treasures of 'nostalgia', as well as my clothes – luggage – shoes and records of holidays I'd so enjoyed.

The helpers included Len Markham who had had a sad divorce since moving to the village and now lived in a rented cottage opposite corner cottage.

Tony, Mark and Pam came with her nephew Jordan who loved unpacking boxes of pots. Jennifer covered carpets with dustsheets, and found a very welcome rug for the kitchen floor. Pam brought one from Cot Nab and they looked fine on the red tiles. Then we used my curtains from the breakfast room. They had been at Burn Butts for Elizabeth and then in her East Leigh bedroom, so this is their third home, which says a lot for Sanderson's fabric! They suit the sitting room too.

Pam whipped down the bright checked pair from the main window, and hung them in the dining end of the kitchen where they looked 'just right'.

The 'Bergere' sofa I'd bought in Harrogate to replace the dowdy one at Witton House in recent years looked as if it was bought specially for the cottage with two easy chairs – my favourites – covered in gold covers, also matched well. Incidentally I paid £500 for the sofa – a bargain as the chairs had been sold. It was the most I'd ever paid for furniture.

There was room for the Davenport desk near the little window and the mahogany side table, which I'd found in an antique shop in York to be a dressing table – now looked 'right' as it did in Witton House sitting room. Now it housed my best cutlery, as I'd left the acorn sideboard, dining table and chairs behind. They meant a lot to Jack, but I always preferred antique furniture and they haven't found a home yet!

Maureen and Jennifer brought my clothes in the evening and we were all fairly straight by bedtime. Daisy was rather bewildered, but slept well in my bedroom, as the kitchen hadn't a door to the hall.

The next day the family were helping again, with fridge (handed on from Mark) and the washer to be fixed by Tony. I'd only made one new purchase for the cottage and that was a little T.V. I have a thing about disliking a T.V. to dominate a room, so this very small model (Pam helped me choose it in Stamford Bridge) suited me well.

Pictures went up (lots of hooks ready in all rooms, hall and landing) Jennifer brought a mirror for the bathroom, and Pam went off to Malton to buy toilet roll holder and towel rails as none left – just marks on the walls!! Also an Aga kettle.

I had lots of cards and flowers. Also lots of visitors including Father Finnemore who made a remark to be quoted in the future "You haven't brought a double bed – what will the Fitzpatricks do when they come?" I replied, "They'll have to manage in adjoining rooms – like the aristocracy!"

The two little spare rooms have single beds alongside a wall as it is, and 'doubles' would have made them crowded.

I prefer a single bed to myself and easier for laundry, bed-making and mattress turning.

Pam and Tony were sleeping at Witton House by now, with Mark and Lisa at Cot Nab. I had Tony and Pam for breakfast on the Sunday, as they hadn't any cereal bowls or cutlery!

Jane and Curly, Pam and Tony later helped to put the little freezer (also from Mark's Fridaythorpe house) in my garage and to sort things from Witton House freezer. Jennifer brought my pots of hydrangeas to put alongside my front garden, which consisted of weeds, wood chippings and two shrubs.

In the middle of moving and getting 'set straight' I had a phone call from Emma Brooksbank with the sad news of the sudden death of her father Lord Holderness.

He had been reluctant to move down to Winkfield, after selling Flat Top House. He had been a great personality in our village for so long (before we moved to Cot Nab) and he was very much missed when they moved.

We had seen a lot of daughter Emma too, in her pony club years. Now she was Lady Brooksbank, married to Nicholas with a son and a daughter.

On Monday August 12th, three days after the move, I was sufficiently settled to have Tom Sloan to stay! His visit had been arranged for Witton House some time ago, but I wrote to say "still come, but to the cottage" and so I welcomed my first visitor!

We had lovely weather and with the garden seat (which Ian had restored and painted a year ago) in my courtyard, and chairs brought from Witton House we could sit out.

Tom took me to Pocklington the next day, and bought me a collection of lamp shades from "A-Z" and they were soon fixed up. I do hate to see bare light bulbs.

Maureen and Barry had been up to Scotland to visit an aged Aunt, and on return he fixed up shelves for me.

William put up the barometer in the hall with the horse brasses on their wooden hangers.

Tom and I went to visit his old friend in West Stansfield, the widow of a former vicar of Gawsworth. We saw her lovely house, and had coffee before going to a pub for lunch. Also while Tom was here we went on a "Parish Outing" with James, and a few others – lunch at Leavening pub. We had a visit from Sarah and Lucy,

Elizabeth Brumfield had been asked to a supper here, but had to refuse after a fall during a funeral service! She had 'blacked out' and cut her lip badly on a pew. It took weeks for this to heal with difficulty in eating.

I was sorry to see Tom go, but there were many jobs to see to. I had to get more used to the Aga for one thing, but once Tony and William had got the temperature right, it wasn't so difficult.

I did find the kitchen far too hot when summer weather was at its best, and had to keep the doors and windows open. Tony sent down a spare fan he had which helped. He said from the first, that I had to use the Aga all the time, no electric kettle or toaster. This seemed sensible to me as he paid the oil bill (as part of my farm pension) and I paid for the electricity!

We all went to the Requiem Mass at Kirby Underdale for Lord Holderness – the church was very full – ushers in morning suits, and I (because of age I'm sure) was shown to a seat. Many were standing. I talked to Emma, her husband and family.

Later on reading the list of mourners I was surprised to see Mary Sheepshanks had been in church. One of my favourite novelists, to whom I'd written on two occasions and she had replied at length. I heard later, Lady Holderness and Emma thought her a lovely person.

Ian had left Woldgate and was working full time at the Medforth's farm at Thixendale and enjoying it much more than school.

Lucy was living with Colin by then, a doctor of science and head of his year at Boroughbridge school. Lucy had a job nursing "in the community" and they bought a house in Harrogate near the showground.

I had plans for my tiny garden at the front, with a few yards of stream (the beck) to look after with the bank overgrown with bindweed. I had help with getting favourite plants from Witton House garden, and re-planting in hot weather. The chippings had to be raked off, and many dandelions dug up, but gradually the neglected plot began to look more cared for.

After harvest, Tony and Mark brought old floor tiles from Cot Nab and laid little paths where I wanted them and a standing for the other seat I'd bought at Langlands. I also moved the stones we'd acquired originally from Wharram Percy! That was before the medieval village was excavated, to become a site of worldwide importance! Near my precious (and historic stones) I put the partly damaged little statue of a girl with plaits which Bunky and Tom had given to me when they sold their lovely home in Bramhall Park.

All the friends and relations who came to see me in the cottage were enthusiastic, saying things like "Its just right for you" or "I love it and you've got it all just as it should be" and so on.

Joan Voase was the only one with many reservations and I don't think it was because she was critical as usual, but more because she wouldn't be as adaptable to changes. I'm lucky in being able to adapt to different surroundings. She seemed worried about my lack of views, and having a small garden or only the courtyard at the back. I don't think she took to the cheerful colours of walls inside either. However, I was glad she was well enough to be driven here by Ken, who also helped to move plants to the front garden.

I enjoyed my daily walk to the shop with Daisy, or to go further to see Eileen. I loved other people's gardens, or going down the 'snicket' near my front door to the lane behind where there are fields, cows and sheep in view. Also the never-ending pleasure of looking up to the Wolds.

This end of the village has a greater population than the Witton House end, so I see far more people, traffic, horses being exercised, dog walkers, and all so friendly.

Jennifer and William are only a hundred yards away, and going on past their house one is soon beyond the village boundary with open countryside.

Tony kept bringing well-loved things for the courtyard, the small, but very old stone trough we'd once found at Manna Green, and the stone geese bought in Pocklington market.

I found the courtyard private, sunny all day in good weather, and was glad not to be rushing around to cope with all the jobs which had become rather an effort at Witton House. Quite simply I was glad to "downsize" even if it meant any large-scale meals were impossible.

I found the Aga a mystery in some ways and no instruction book – just a few hints from Pam as to ways of reducing temperature for cakes and biscuits. I got a heavy solid shelf, which could be slotted in at the top of the hot oven, and I found I could check on a cake after a time, before moving it to the low oven.

Sometimes I forgot the shelf was there and couldn't understand why pastry didn't brown or roast potatoes stayed un-crisp.

Two advantages were not having fumes when cooking, and ovens that didn't need cleaning.

This Aga is old and the top surface has been badly treated at some time so the glossy effect is marred and unpolishable! Tony being an Aga perfectionist, even if he doesn't cook, told me to keep the top plates clean and bright, "never trail a pan from one ring to the other, and don't stand anything on the plates at all". I soon found the hot, bright covering 'tops' were ideal for ironing and I took great delight in not having to get out the iron and heavy ironing board, except for more intricate garments like dresses or fussy blouses. Just by folding, pressing with the hands and turning, I get satisfactory results and ideal for sheets of course.

The heat of the Aga was a problem with glasses stored over it on shelves or nearby cupboards. I have to cool down a water jug for instance, or table glasses, but I am glad dinner plates didn't need warming.

After many months I found more storage space in the second-hand shop in Pocklington. Two bedside cabinets – well made in Melamine – open shelves with 2 drawers. I thought, 'I can stand one on top of the other over the fridge in the awkward corner away from the Aga.' I bought them and friends who called that day helped to collect and put them in place. Perfectly balanced, they were safe and looked tidy and were so useful in a kitchen lacking cupboard space!

By the end of September Jim and Mary Fitz came to stay, and loved it. They even managed in separate bedrooms!

One afternoon sitting in sun in the courtyard we had unexpected visitors. First Pam, Jane and baby Laura, followed by Elizabeth Bunting and Jane Burchell (my ex neighbour), so we had quite a party for cool drinks. Elizabeth Bunting was visiting family (Towthorpe Megginsons) so was welcome especially as we seldom see her.

We had a lovely visit with Jim and Mary. Mary even went to the W.I. with me, while Jim took Daisy for a walk.

Next day we drove to Fraisthorpe, where they met Mary Jackson after

I'd had a swim. We all had so many memories of Fraisthorpe in the war years when we first met Jim and Mary.

My next-door neighbour Isobel had a 10 lb baby boy the next day – her first!

I went to York with the Fitz's – "Park and Ride" but I think Jim found it a tiring day.

Maureen and Barry were at Dryden Cottage where we had an evening meal.

I was sorry to see the Fitz's leave.

One day I went with Eileen to Pocklington and I bought lino for the back porch to cover the painted floor. It was quite heavy carrying to the car, but I managed. I soon had it cut and laid, feeling quite proud of my effort.

Another day that autumn, Bill Derrick Sykes came to see the cottage and me. After lunch we went to Fraisthorpe, which he didn't know at all, drove down to see Kingsfield and on to North Kingsfield where Frank Milner saw us – invited us in for coffee and cake! Again many memories when the Milner family were our neighbours.

They have made great alterations to the old house, and added an extension. Also the farm buildings are now very top class holiday cottages! Very different from their parents' time.

David and Shirley Allison were leaving the village shop in October. I made them a card with verse – we had a farewell party at Anne Sumpners – the village shop is so important, especially to non-drivers like me, and we were all glad it was to continue with the new owners Alex and Wendy still living in adjoining house.

Later that year I had a holiday in Cheshire with Tom and we had good walks before we went to Chester garden centre where we met the Fitz's and I went on to stay with them at the 'Nant' for the last time. We celebrated their Diamond Wedding with a wonderful midday Mass for twenty three friends – their great friend 'The Canon' had stayed overnight (a charming man) and took the service. Afterwards I read a verse I'd written for the occasion, and we enjoyed a buffet lunch.

The next day I returned by trains from Chester, Jennifer met me at York and Daisy hadn't been any bother.

Soon after that Roy and Roz came for the day and it was lovely to see them and their first visit to the cottage.

Coidy came for a few days, looking very smart, straight from attending "Women of the Year" lunch in London at the Savoy!

During her visit we went to charity shops in Pocklington and I found a smart Jersey suit in the Hospice Shop for Lucy's wedding.

Jennifer and William made a great effort and drove Coidy back to Cheltenham, returning the same day!

Lucy married Colin Lefley on October 19th and I went with Maureen and Barry to Harrogate registry office, and to a meal at the White Hart Hotel. All very happy, and we saw them off to the Lake District from their home later in the day.

In November Maureen and I went via Harrogate to Lucy's degree ceremony at Sheffield University. She can now put 'B.Sc. – Nursing Science', after her name!

Maureen, Barry, Ian and I went to Rachel and Norman's grave at Mappleton. Never a happy place to visit, but we feel we must go twice a year. Ian was still working for the Medforths at Thixendale at that time.

One day in November Joan drove here herself – the first time since March and had a fish pie meal with me.

Events like the Kirby Underdale Dinner took place. This year a 'Tartan' theme, and a very successful evening – last year had been 'Black and White'. I helped by cleaning and preparing a bucket of parsnips from Witton House garden, grown by Ian. There were 50 people to feed for a four course meal.

I was making 'trogs' – in spare time to sell at the church bazaar, as Jennifer brought one from Norway with the idea of me copying it, and they sold well.

I had a lunch of jacket potatoes, sausages and apple pie for helpers when we decided to abandon the traditional Friday evening bazaar for a Saturday morning effort. It worked well with more than £800 raised.

By the time I had to decorate for Christmas I suffered from pulled muscles, which were very painful. Tony helped to string a great many cards on the beams and got the tree lights going.

I was so lame after Midnight Mass with backache, that Nancie and Moira helped me walk home. 2 a.m. by the time I got to bed with aspirin. Christmas Day I improved a bit, with family calling, Tony, Pam, Ian, Mark and Lisa for coffee – then to Jennifer's for drinks and called at the Quarmby's before going to Maureen and Barry's with all Mo's family for a wonderful turkey meal - games etc and home 8 p.m. for T.V. and sleep!

On Boxing Day I felt much better and went to Becca and Geoff's – Sally, Christopher and Nicola were there too in Norton so another happy family day.

I managed to accommodate and feed 16 of family the following Sunday for a meal late afternoon. Rather a squash, but we coped, and I felt pleased to be able to keep up 'family party' tradition.

Jennifer drove me to Elizabeth Brumfield for a New Year lunch and so ended my first Christmas at Corner Cottage!

2003 started off with very icy weather – also I suffered from a bad back. I missed a 'panto' trip, but went to a party at Mo and Barry's – twenty guests. I got a lift both ways and the diary tells me I was forbidden to venture out on the very slippery roads!

Daisy was walked by Jen mostly. Even the W.I. A.G.M. was cancelled because of ice! I managed to get the Christmas decorations down and Mo helped by taking them to store in the garage.

One afternoon I had Elizabeth (nee Beaulah) to see me, bringing Connie Beaulah who was beginning to fail in mind and body.

I asked Tony to come to see Elizabeth, who has lived in Australia for many years, and she seems to love meeting up with old friends in Yorkshire and to talk of Cot Nab years when the Beaulahs were good neighbours.

The bad icy spell lasted for half of January. Tony would be sixty on 19th and we were trying to find him a garden seat from us all.

They had bought "The Stables" – a converted barn at Skirpenbeck, so at last they had the move to look forward to.

By Tony's birthday I had developed a bad chest infection. I remember being so short of breath I had to sit on the village seat before going to the shop – so once again I couldn't walk Daisy.

Tony had a lunch party at 'Prospect House' in Gate Helmsley – where they had good caterers in the large conservatory. Jen and William had the garden seat in their 'Discovery Land Rover'.

I had little appetite, but sat between Barry and John Cartledge so could 'off load' meat and vegetables. After the meal we went to Cot Nab for cake in the shape of a Range Rover.

I should have read at a carol service at Bugthorpe that afternoon, but was not well enough.

I had to cancel other things, and by January 23rd Jen called a doctor and I was put on antibiotics!

Lorna Sleightholme fell in her kitchen and broke her hip, and had a long spell of recovery after an operation for replacement.

February started with snow – and I went to lunch at Limetree (Jennifer and William's home) with Sally and children, and Rebecca with Sophie. Children had fun playing in the snow.

Witton House was advertised in the "Property" Supplement of Yorkshire Post £387,000 (I think!) and Jack paid £32,000 all those years ago!

Ian was working at Medforths, but came down one afternoon with terrier Smidge. He was happily having driving lessons and as usual I was delighted to see him.

We were sad when John Stringer died – we had all been close friends in the Cot Nab years – with many happy memories of the times with the Stringer family at High Callis.

There was a very full church for his memorial service – and by mistake and through helping Lily to count the collection, and putting chairs away, I missed getting a lift up to Callis Wold afterwards. I felt sorry to miss that. A few days later Martin phoned and called to see me – along with Nigel Cottam and his wife Elizabeth (nee Stringer).

Ian passed his driving test easily and went with Jennifer and Tony for an interview at Harper Adams Agricultural College in Staffordshire. Later it was known as a University!

That springtime passed in usual activities – mostly village affairs – and when the W.I. cleaned out the beck on a Sunday in March, I had Pam and a few others for coffee in the courtyard as fine and sunny.

March 21st William and Jennifer set off for Cumbria for William to start the 'Coast-to-Coast' walk, which he completed. They had the caravan with Jennifer being a 'ferry' vehicle for meeting William and getting him back.

Joan was still quite well and came for lunch on two occasions – with a short walk afterwards.

I had a lovely day with Hilary Mason when Nancie Boyes took me to Sherburn while she visited her daughter in Scarborough. Hilary and I always have so much to talk about when we do manage to meet with memories of horsey years with our families.

I often went to Pocklington with Eileen to do some shopping and one day Daisy went too for her "shampoo and trim" which seemed expensive at £16, but she looked so smart afterwards.

We had extra church services throughout Lent, and on Palm Sunday a procession with Donkey and Tom Farrow lead her round the church afterwards.

Jane Megginson collected me from church to go to the 80th birthday lunch in Malton for Steve Megginson. My coat had hairs on it from hugging the donkey! There were 70 people there, and 'finger buffet' so I didn't feel hungry when Jane dropped me off at the village hall here on our return for Bernard Hutchinson's 80th which took the form of an old style type of Yorkshire tea party.

On April 25th Elizabeth and I set off from York Station for a train journey to Inverness to join the ship "Lord of the Isles" on a cruise down the

Caledonian Canal. I thought how easy to just sit on the train all that way, but at Perth we came to a standstill with engine trouble! We all had to get out with no advice about platforms or relief train! We were thankful that a kind young man helped us with our luggage. We "hung about" and sat on the platform for an hour being helped on to another train, which had in our carriage – a noisy party on a 'stag-night' in Aviemore. Elizabeth had to call the Station Hotel in Inverness on her mobile phone to say we would be late for dinner, difficult to hear through all the noise, but we gathered we could only be served cold food!

Eventually we arrived in Inverness and the lovely young man even carried our cases into the hotel foyer where Elizabeth was thankful to have a large brandy before our salad meal!

We were very ready for our baths and beds! After the difficult start we explored the town next morning and in the afternoon met up with fellow passenger Margaret who became a true friend. We had a wonderful cruise to Oban, with spectacular scenery on the way and very interesting excursions from the ship. I learned much Scottish history with also a day on Mull and Iona. I have 'written up' this holiday as I have recorded all the others I've been fortunate to enjoy.

Life in Corner Cottage proceeded with various callers and seeing people. I took Elizabeth to the Fleece on her birthday and we walked round back lanes afterwards.

There was a 'surprise party' for Elizabeth Hodgson's 70th at Bolton Hall Farm. Twelve guests (including Tony and Pam) and Ruth and Robert served a very good three-course meal.

The day (May 18th) ended with a happy phone call from Maureen with the news of a baby girl "Hannah" for Lucy and Colin.

Maureen, Sarah and I went to see the new babe the next day in Harrogate Hospital and had a good meal later at Dryden Cottage before going to the local Parish Council meeting. The Diary records "19 spectators and Fiona did well," but I've really no recollection of what it was all about!

Joan came for the day again and after lunch we went to the supermarket in Pocklington for a few things we wanted, but she was never keen about shopping and got as little as possible.

Ian came for a hot meal as Tony and Pam were on a short holiday to see friends in the Liverpool area.

Mickey came to stay in June after arranging a meeting and lunch with her daughter Ali near Hardwick Hall. Tony who drove had also to go to a place in Derbyshire to get his caravan mattresses re-stuffed.

After all that we were back by 3.30, and Tony took us to Cot Nab to have tea and biscuits with Mark as Pam not there. Tony gave Mickey a tour of vintage Range Rovers, and we saw Mark's racing car, which he was restoring.

While Mickey was here we went round the charity shops and met Elizabeth Brumfield by chance in Pocklington, so she treated us to a café lunch before driving us to see her lovely garden at Seaton Ross where we could sit in the sun and eat cake before being driven back.

We really had a treat on the Monday in very good weather, as we went with Maureen and Jennifer to Castle Howard for the outdoor performance of 'Toad of Toad Hall' by the Park Lane Company from Leeds.

Luckily Mickey and I had a shooting stick and another seat-stick to rest on as there was a lot of walking up and down hills, and through woodland – up to the "Temple of the Four Winds"(the court scene up there) and it was all really enchanting.

There weren't many adults in the audience, but two very well behaved groups of young school children. We specially loved Badger's house in the wood with 'wild wooders' climbing trees and shrieking down to us. The caravan horse "Alfred" reminded me of my efforts as his front legs in convent days.

The finale was wonderful and held in the back hall of the castle itself, with riotous 'wild wooders' holding a drunken banquet before the fight in which Toad, Mole, Badger and Ratty were victorious.

It was all quite magical and Mickey and I felt we'd really had a great treat and couldn't stop talking about it.

The family have always been so good about helping out with visitors and the visitors always remark on their friendly help. This time Tony took Mickey home, as he and Pam were going to a Range Rover rally in the Northants area.

Not long after that (almost immediately) Coidy was brought here, and enjoyed her stay. I noticed she had failed in some ways; sight, hearing and a bit unsteady when out. One afternoon she decided to walk to the shop to buy chocolates to take to dear 'old' Eileen. However, she felt faint on the way and had to be revived with cups of tea and was driven back here by Eileen!

Jennifer and I had a good day out with the Farm Women's Club, also in June and we went to Alnwick Castle – the gardens will be a real show place and tourist attraction, but we felt they need to mature.

Jennifer got stung by a bee down her blouse, when we were in the garden! Luckily I had some "Bite Ease" in my bag, but the sting bothered her for some time after. The castle was lovely, a very fine situation. I always like the F.W.C. ladies, so friendly and all with a common interest.

What a busy month! I went to stay with Tom, by train and was met at Manchester airport. I had a pleasant two days in Gawsworth and met Chris, Liz and David for a pub meal. We also saw "Merry Wives of Windsor" at the open-air theatre in Gawsworth and then went, next day to meet the Fitzs at the Grosvenor Garden Centre.

Tom drove back home after a pleasant lunch and I went on to Llanrhaedr with Jim and Mary to their new little house with a wonderful view down the garden to the river with sheep and cows on the bank.

We called on their friend Chris on the small farm where she was dying of cancer. Her nice husband had died since my last visit. Seeing Chris so ill, reminded me of Rachel at that stage.

I was invited to join in a local evening party in the village - mostly in the garden, with 160 guests and entertainment, and a wonderful buffet meal. The Welsh are so friendly – contrary to general opinion of people who don't live there! The Fitzs had been encouraged to leave the "Nant" by my 'downsize' move.

I had some lovely drives in beautiful countryside before coming home and a good train journey.

Jennifer had been worried about her dear dog Muffy (Wire Haired German Pointer) and had to have the vet when on a caravan holiday in Rosedale. Soon after she died of liver cancer. This was a great blow and Jennifer was so sad to lose such a charming, amusing dog at a young age.

We all helped with the 'Scarecrow' weekend in the village. I concocted a female to sit on my beck side bank. I stuffed an old jumper and skirt with rags, and old newspapers and made legs from stuffed tights, with the 'feet' ending in wellies. A mop for hair and a rakish hat completed the figure. Oh yes, I used pink 'briefs' for the face and painted on features. The most difficult part was joining the head to body with a scarf, but as the woman was supposed to be drunk, it didn't matter if it flopped. With an empty wine bottle and a balloon strung to the hedge, I added a label "the morning after the night before".

I put a child with pigtails, a wide brimmed hat, and a teddy on my garden seat, as it all made interest for the many passers by!

There were some wonderful creations up and down the village.

We had a rota of helpers selling programmes in the centre of the village and Rector James thought we should dress up as scarecrows! He phoned on the Sunday morning to ask if I'd do a 'stint' – so I hurriedly had to dress myself in an old raincoat with a pole across the sleeves – stuffed with greenery I'd gathered which hung out at the sleeve ends.

I pulled an old felt hat down over my face, buttoned myself into the mac and walked off down the street, to the surprise of onlookers, or passers by!

We had a very successful weekend financially and socially, and provided continuous refreshments. Needless to say, lots of hard work to organise it all.

There was a heat wave in mid July and I really enjoyed the hot sun, but the Aga made the cottage hot even with a fan, and doors and windows open.

Very hot for the family picnic at Levisham which was especially good on July 13th. Forty one of us, and children played well and in the stream, and we had the usual walk to the station to see the steam trains.

We got home by early evening, and I phoned Ken for news of poor Joan who had had a bad fall down stairs two days before and was now in Hull Royal.

Joan improved very slowly, but with not much interest in anything from Ken's reports and not wanting to walk with nurses' help and couldn't bother to read my letters.

I felt sorry at not being able to visit her, but the family were busy, though I did get for a day on the beach at Filey and had a swim as Katy drove me to meet Pam, Jane and Laura who were at Cayton with caravan.

I talked to Heather about Joan in the evening. At last on July 23rd I went to see Joan, as Elizabeth Hodgson was driving Nancie to visit Gordon Foster in the same hospital. It was quite difficult to find Joan's ward. She was lying down, fully dressed on her bed – pleased to see me, but said she hadn't much interest in anything – I don't think she read the almost daily letters and cards I'd sent. I asked about the plans for her to go home very soon, and about the chair lift already installed. She said, "I don't seem able to think about it at all".

As I was leaving she gave me a lovely smile and said "You do look nice!" and I came away thinking I'd soon be visiting her at Baswick.

The next day, Friday 24th Ken phoned with news of her sudden death! I was so glad I'd been to see her, and felt perhaps it was better that she hadn't been at home as an invalid, as I'm sure she wouldn't have been happy.

I had a lovely day soon after, visiting Harewood House with Elizabeth H, with daughter Ruth and little Naomi. The grounds were wonderful, and I went alone to look round the fascinating house, my first time there. Before leaving it, I was in the hall when two elderly people got out of a car on the drive and walked into the hall and through a private door. They were easily recognisable as Lord and Lady Harewood.

I bought a good book written by him after his 80th birthday.

On July 27th Heather phoned to ask if I would speak about Joan at the funeral on Thursday 31st. I agreed to do this, and sat in the sun, in the courtyard thinking of Joan's life and all the many years, of a close friendship since we were six years old. Joan and Pam part of our 'Corner Quartet' in our form in convent days. Now only Mickey and I left.

Later over the next day or two, I wrote down the words for the eulogy.

Tony and Pam drove me and Jen and William to Brandesburton church for the funeral. A nice service, with hymns Joan would have liked. My eulogy went well, if difficult to deliver, but I coped with it, and afterwards they all seemed grateful for it. I got a laugh too – in illustrating how Joan's outspoken remarks often covered her concern for others.

Afterwards, at Baswick – dear Ken was quite distressed, but it was lovely to meet all the family, including Barbara and Bill from Weymouth where Joan and I once stayed together and to be in the garden. The family provided very good refreshments, or perhaps they had caterers?

We got home by early evening, and I phoned Joan Laughton to report on the funeral.

On the following Sunday, which would have been Joan's birthday, Olga Voase, her daughter-in-law, collected me at midday to go to Baswick for a lunch party, and to scatter Joan's ashes on the rose bed.

A pleasant afternoon with the family all there, and fine enough to be in the garden all the time.

I know Joan loved her roses, but I don't think I would like my ashes so near the house, but then I don't really want a 'ceremony' as such at all!

Early August was so hot, that on the 5th Jen took me to the beach at Fraisthorpe, for a picnic – sunbathing, rest and I had a swim. William had said, "The beach is for children", but Jen replied it was much easier just to take her old Mother!

On August 11th we had a storm, and water ran down the road like a river. However Tom Sloan drove here in good weather conditions, and arrived at 2.30 for cold beer in the courtyard.

Jennifer and William were in Swaledale, but Maureen called to see Tom with Alison. One day on his visit he drove over the Wolds, and we stopped at North Grimston for lunch (I remember a very heavy treacle sponge) and then as far as Sherburn and Weaverthorpe.

We also had a lovely time at Fraisthorpe when Jane Megginson came to drive us after having a cold salmon lunch here. We took a flask and biscuits for later and they laughed at my antics of undressing on the beach before a swim.

We talked to Mary Jackson at the farm, and then drove down to South Kingsfield and also North and saw the Milners, this meeting again bringing back memories of my early married life.

On return Tony and Pam came for an evening meal and 'all left by 11 p.m.' so quite a day! The Diary also mentions 'letter in Women's Post' that week and again 'letter in Yorkshire Post'. Tom and I took some 'Jack' books to Forths in Pocklington – so still selling them.

Tom left early morning and had a good drive back. Looking to later years, it was the last time he was able to drive here.

Maureen and Barry were due to move to a semi-detached 'bungalow' with good 'upstairs' in Cayton.

We would miss Maureen in the village, but Dryden Cottage needed improvements and they were finding two houses difficult to keep up.

Maureen said "near the sea" if she had to leave Bishop Wilton, and as Barry worked in Scarborough – his hometown – they looked in that area.

Cayton proved a good choice and the first day they had the key I went to see it with Sarah and David. We had a picnic in the garden and found it all very pleasant.

We walked later to the bay which I only remembered pre-war! It is still very unspoilt and a steep path down to the beach – views of Scarborough Castle and very secluded and quiet.

The next day I went with Elizabeth Brumfield driven by Peter to Nantwich to join the boat, the Buty – but it had changed names so it was rather confusing when looking for it on the canal. Now "Duke and Duchess" with David and Mother in charge. As I've written this holiday up elsewhere, I'll just say it was a lovely week and scenery especially good, finishing in Llangollen! The aqueduct crossing had been very impressive. While we were away Mo and Barry moved to Cayton.

On September 3rd, Jen, William, with friends Stephen and Ann flew to Canada and on the 7th Ian was 18.

Later that month, the Fitz's arrived – pleased by journey and we sat in the courtyard and talked before having a cold lunch and then a walk.

Lucy, Sarah, Alison and Hannah arrived and later in evening a meal with extra table needed as Dave and Colin came to put their spare fridge and bookcase in store. Sarah now shared her cottage with Dave, brother to Colin.

All the family came to see the Fitzs during this visit, except Jen and William of course. With Maureen and Barry working we had a seaside day and ate our picnic in their garden and looked round the house.

After that week, life continued as usual in the village. My good neighbours Isobel and John had left me in charge of their budgie while in Cornwall with young Sid and the dogs.

On September 7th I went to Cayton with Dave, Sarah and Alison. A lovely day, only spoilt by news of Alison losing her job. This proved to be the last of her private-nanny-live in jobs, and it meant having to find other accommodation.

Eventually she got a nursery job in York and shared a house with friends. It was a pity as the last job provided a nice little flat, but apart from that, the parents made life difficult, though she loved the children.

We had a good sunny day, with our first meal in the dining room – good roast lamb and afterwards a walk to the lovely, unspoilt beach, with steep path down and up!

That evening – Ian's 18th birthday - Barry, Maureen and I joined others at Millington pub for a celebration meal. With friends Robert and Colwen – as well as family.

On the 12th September, Pam, Elizabeth H and I had been to the cinema in Hull to see the famous W.I. film, inspired by the Rylstone ladies in memory of one of their husband's death from Leukaemia. They made more than a million eventually for research. A feat that inspired us all and made the film an international success.

A few weeks later I enjoyed the film just as much in Pocklington at the Arts Centre.

There were always village and church duties to fit in and I enjoyed my frequent visits to call on Eileen with Daisy, after the morning visit to the shop.

After a session of sewing name tapes on a dozen pairs of boxer shorts bought in Pocklington market for Ian, we drove down in two cars to take him and all necessary luggage, even a fridge – to settle him in at Harper Adams in Shropshire.

I was in Ian's car and he drove very well and with confidence.

Ian went in to register, while Tony and I had a walk round, and watched many parents with new students.

Afterwards we helped carry things to Ian's 'en-suite' apartment and found Pam had forgotten sheets, so we went into Newport and quite easily found a shop and bought two sets.

We had drinks and a snack with Ian and then left him, looking a bit forlorn as we set off on the four-hour drive home.

A day later he phoned, and sounded settled, and gave a list of more things needed for his room!

Decorating the church for 'Harvest' was something I no longer looked forward to – did I ever? But it was easier when younger, and with more helpers, that year it was rather an effort.

However, there was Susan English's 80th birthday to cheer me up.

Susan's family arranged it all at the "Gateway to York" Hotel and I went with Nancie, Lorna and Eileen. Thirty guests, a good company with the English family and old friends like Bunty Megginson with her zimmer and Peter and Joan Atkinson looking older, like a lot of us.

Later that day I helped to get the village hall ready for the Harvest tea party, and on the Sunday was part of the team to prepare food.

There was a choir from Orchard Park in Hull where James's friend is a priest and the children enjoyed the food. There were readings (I did one) and the evening passed pleasantly.

I look back to earlier Harvest celebration services, when farmers and work people all attended, and when it all seemed more like working and praying together in a close community.

William and Jennifer were back from holiday in Canada with their friends, the Derbyshires, but had missed the party and 'Harvest'. Jennifer came round to report on the holiday and gave me a lovely canvas shopping bag with animal designs – I am still making good use of it and it has often been admired.

Jen and William soon collected the Rough Haired German Pointer pup they called Libby. I went with them as the kennels were near Horncastle where we had lunch with Roy Layzell (Pam's widower) in his lovely bungalow in Woodhall Spa. There was much distress and worry over this pup before she grew up. A dear dog, as Muffy had been.

I enjoyed giving a talk to the Probis Club in York, on the 'Farm Lads' – I also often had friends for easy lunches (I never did roasts after coming here – not much space and carving not easy). I had Ken Voase, Harold and Jean, Hilary Mason and Derrick Sykes at various times.

Ian drove up one weekend, very cheerful and coping well in his new life. He collected utensils etc needed for his college room.

It was good to meet David Butterworth with Duff Peacock for lunch at the Fleece and afterwards they came here for coffee. David had been a worry to us all with so long an illness. I was pleased to keep in touch and recently had gone with Jean Megginson to have lunch with Robert Peacock at Howe Bridge Farm – home of his son Graham and daughter-in-law Rosa who also farm in New Zealand. When Maureen and I were in N.Z. with Lucy we had a wonderful day on the farm there, and a proper meal at a dining table. A change from our 'camping style' while there.

I was fascinated too by Rosa's grandparents and family history in general after emigrating from Devon, but I may have written of that before.

I was glad to go to the October lunch in 2003, and it was lovely to meet Robert too. He had been such a close friend to Jack in their young schooldays at Wharram village school, under the efficient teaching of Miss Wallace.

We ate roast venison at Howe Bridge as they had a lot in the woods near the farm. It reminded me of staying in Somerset years ago with Rachel's friends who were 'Annie's' parents the Earles in their unique old house with wood panelled walls, a porch of heather thatch, and numerous pictures and photos. Chrystal Earle also cooked venison for Jack and me! I think the first time we'd eaten it. Later Annie was godmother to Ian.

Village life went on much as usual walking Daisy, seeing Eileen, Elizabeth Hodgson and Nancie. Also Ken Voase came to lunch about once a month and perhaps Jane Cartledge would call with Laura. Jean and Harold sometimes came over from Malton and I had a day in London by train with Bill Derrick to see an old friend who lived in a flat in the wonderful Charterhouse College. I found it all fascinating and we were shown all round. Sid, an artist in his working life entertained us well, after lunch in a nearby French restaurant.

There was a snag on the way back with the First Class train, seats comfortable, but serious delays, which got worse, and at Peterborough we had to change trains and eventually arrived in York about three hours late with taxis in demand as no connections to Malton or Scarborough. We got one by 1 a.m. and were ready for our beds at Poppleton!

Coidy had now failed in health, sight and hearing. So wanting to keep in touch with her Yorkshire friends, she took to booking in at the excellent care home Larchfield in Harrogate. She was president of the English Speaking Board, and her mind and speech as lively as ever. She was well known for having written a very good novel with Yorkshire background, at the age of ninety.

Jennifer and I visited her one day in October and had lunch in an annexe to the main dining room, so easier for conversation.

I think we have now been four times to see Coidy at Larchfield – and have had amusing moments including visits to her favourite charity shops where she shares my talent for finding good clothes at low prices.

In November, Colin and Helen Newlove called one evening – their first visit to the Cottage, though Colin phoned regularly for a chat – full of amusing anecdotes and enthusiasms as usual.

It was always a pleasure to have Maureen for supper, bed and breakfast on Thursdays, when she worked in Pocklington at "Take it Easy" till 7 p.m., so often hungry by the time she got here.

Sometimes Tony and or Jennifer dropped in to see her, and she often went for an early morning walk in the village before a meagre breakfast, as felt she lacked exercise in this job.

As usual in the weeks before our church Bazaar in early December I was making things to sell – we now had it on a Saturday morning rather than Friday evenings, as in times remembered way back, and it has proved a good idea. However, I have quite a rush as I started the custom of having a few helpers including my stall helper Peggy Lecuas for a hot lunch afterwards.

There was the usual so called "run up" to Christmas and we had snow on December 22nd more near coast, and Maureen had to turn back at Octon crossroads.

The previous weekend Maureen and Barry had stayed here overnight for a party at the Machins.

I decorated my little tree and put garlands up the banisters etc. calling on Eileen I found her with more pain in her foot, so I got coal in for her.

On Christmas Eve, I was invited to two parties! Moira's and Fiona's. I had been busy packing for Daisy and me to go to Cayton for Christmas. We arrived before midnight and found Lucy walking round with baby Hannah!

Christmas day was lovely! Barry cooked a breakfast of scrambled eggs with smoked salmon, after getting up early to butter the turkey! Then, a present opening session, before Maureen, Barry and I went to church where the vicar was lively and amusing.

Colin, Lucy and Hannah had a long walk with a rather tired Daisy! Later we had a rest and Maureen, Lucy and I went to Scarborough sea front, and I stayed with Hannah sleeping in the car while they walked.

We had a wonderful late meal, and played games till bedtime.

On Boxing Day morning, I took Daisy for quite a long walk in the very cold weather. Dave, Sarah and Alison joined us and there was more present opening. Tony and Pam arrived for coffee and mince pies, then Jennifer, William, Katy and Cameron.

Jennifer and William took me on to Malton and we had drinks at Rebecca's – yes more presents! Jane, Rebecca's friend, Stephen and children were also there and we had a lovely meal – children's games later and after clearing up in kitchen we found Adam (the chief culprit

I think) had fired a shooting thing on to the walls! This caused some consternation, but no serious harm was done! We got home about 6 o'clock – quite tired!

The following Sunday in frosty weather, which made everything look beautiful, I took Daisy on a field walk, and was late for church, as I'd forgotten it was a 10.30 service. I could hear Derek Hodgson's service in the porch before going in. Derek, a retired vicar often helped with our services. I wore my long red coat with Rachel's "Leopard" collar, and Lord Halifax admired it, and asked if it was a Christmas present? I think it stood out as so many of congregation were in dreary black, or dark colours, and where did I buy it? In a shop run for a village church!

We had a "drinks and nibbles" party at the Rectory afterwards with about 20 there.

Later after watching "Alice in Wonderland" on T.V. I phoned Joan Laughton who sounded to have had a lonely Christmas – I am so lucky!

The next day I was collected for a party in Seaton Ross by Elizabeth's friends Keith and Audrey. Elizabeth provided the usual perfect meal and the two new vicars were good company. I was brought home at midnight!

Jennifer and William gave a lovely roast beef meal on December 30th with Becca, Geoff, Sophie and Ian who came to collect me and helped to carry stuff I'd provided as the road was so icy.

There was so much ice on New Year's Eve that earlier in the day Jennifer had taken Daisy out for me. I had an 'old ladies' tea party and cars had to be brought to the door! Lorna, Elizabeth H, Eileen and Nancie.

That evening Maureen and Barry came for the night as invited to the Lindsay-Curtis's for the usual village New Year dinner party. They didn't get in till 4 a.m. after letting out Jen's dogs in snow – as they were away.

So ended 2003.

2004 – The New Year snow didn't last long and I gave a family party on Sunday January 4th. I'd done 'sausage plaits' the night before, and puddings and on the day Jennifer helped bringing jacket potatoes, extra glasses and crockery.

It was all the usual squash in this small house, but we coped well, and all went off happily. The first guests came 3 p.m. and the rest, 20 in all, came along gradually. All left by 9.30, and all cleared up. A few days later I found a forgotten sausage plait all black at the back of the oven!

Sally's new friend and partner, Jeff, was brave enough to face all the family at once, more or less. They were to marry the following May.

We are lucky to have the cinema at Oak House in 'Pock' and Jane

Megginson came later in January and we saw the film of Peter Pan. I never tire of it, but although good in parts – Peter especially, like all modern versions of old classics they become too noisy, with lighting and technical improvements (so called) spoiling the production.

The snow came back suddenly one evening, when Jane was here again to go with Jennifer and William to see the "Calendar Girls" film, my third time – and all enjoyed it. But – on coming out of Oak House there had been a snowfall, and all the way back driving snow was blowing against the windscreen. Jane got worried about driving back to her house in Dunnington, so Jennifer suggested she should stay overnight with them.

Next morning, we walked up to the shop with so many people out, enjoying the unusual snowy scene in sunshine.

Jennifer and Jane had coffee with me before Jane set off home, after watching the dustbin lorry nearly ending up in the beck when trying to negotiate the narrow road to pass the Chestnuts.

It was a difficult morning for Pam at Cot Nab, although she and Tony were sleeping at Witton House still. They had invited me to lunch at Cot Nab with Ken Voase and John and Joan Barmby. Tony collected me after he had been using his snowplough all night.

Pam hadn't really thought there was any hurry to cook the meal as no one would get there, but there was very little snow on the coast, and all three turned up in good time.

We sat round the kitchen table, and chatted for some time, with Pam cooking frantically, though in reality Pam is seldom frantic and gets on with jobs very calmly!

However, no more snow fell, and Pam's roast beef and 'Yorkshires' and puddings to follow went down very well. John and Joan hadn't been round Cot Nab house for many years, so were very keen to see it. They had started their married life in what was the "cottage" end when we moved in 1956. So they were having their dinner in what was their living room.

On February 2nd we heard that contracts on Witton House had been exchanged, and it had to be emptied by the following week! Panic Stations! After the long, long wait, and various false hopes of a sale, there was now a rush!

So much stuff to sort out! Some sent into storage at Cot Nab house, and in the buildings. All things which I might want, some which I had looked forward to having here, and many we hardly new what to do with needed sorting.

Jane helped Pam a lot, and many unwanted items had to got to a tip, or to charity shops. We had left Witton House looking furnished and attractive to buyers and now it had to be empty.

Tony and Pam kept arriving with boxes, pictures, spare small furniture, and so on to put in my garage. I also spread many good pieces of pottery, glass and ornaments on a spare room bed, for members of the family to choose anything they fancied.

The landing was stacked with books, for which I had little space, but I was pleased to have two long mirrors I'd missed, and a hanging set of shelves with little cupboard was fixed on my bedroom wall.

Tony walked in one day with my brass fender from the sitting room and I said "Oh No!" hoping it wouldn't fit round my hearth, but it did, so I had another piece of brass to clean!

Ian sold his pine dresser which had been filling a space in the breakfast room, also a table I think, to Mr and Mrs Minion the new owners so that solved one problem.

Pam hoovered all the carpets before leaving, but with great speed it seemed, most were out on a bonfire across the beck as the workmen there were clearing the site, and rebuilding the old house where we had watched Mary Rowley caring for her bit of land over the years. Mary looked rather masculine and visitors to us looking out from our windows were surprised to know that the 'old man' scything the grass with great skill was an oldish lady!

The fairly new sitting room carpet, I had bought after Jack died, had luckily been rolled up and stored in William's barn.

The Minions had floors in downstairs rooms polished and left bare, but the hall floor boards were not good enough, so were covered with checked vinyl floor covering. Later they made much needed improvements to the old house.

I resorted to a 'garage sale' in aid of the new village hall one Saturday morning, and got rid of some surplus stuff like that. My neighbours from the "Chestnuts" also brought a table full of things they offered for sale.

It was rather disconcerting to find some objects I'd had around my homes for years were unwanted at 50p! Also the odd picture or household objects were of no interest to anyone!

The books I gradually got rid of. I had been especially concerned about my collection of old pre-war theatrical books and plays. Re-reading them again, at least dipping in to odd ones convinced me of the changes in what appeals to the public now compared with pre-war for instance. I eventually gave these books of plays to the Park Lane College in Leeds and they were very grateful.

As Mark and partner, Lisa, were living at Cot Nab, Tony and Pam resorted to renting a small flat in Market Weighton until they eventually signed up for a barn conversion at Skirpenbeck. Four bedrooms, a large kitchen, living room and "dining hall" with conservatory seemed ideal for them within a ten-minute drive to Cot Nab. It was, however, December before they could move in, so not an easy time for them.

There were three 'conversions' close together, the other two larger – so much to do in sowing lawns, fighting issues with "Hare the Builder" and trying to get "The Stables" to their liking on limited funds.

The last conversion wasn't finished until the end of 2005. Luckily Tony and Pam had good "next door" neighbours in the Robinson family and although close, are not overlooked in any way.

In March Tony, now was laid low at the Market Weighton flat by his usual back trouble – and on March 4th Jane and Curly had a baby brother Edward for Laura.

I went with Tony recovered to see them in Bolton when home with the new baby a day or two later.

I had a few nice 'outings' around that date, over to lunch with Steve and Doreen Meg in Malton, going with Jane Meg, and the day before my birthday I went with Jennifer to Cayton – Rebecca was also there and we had a good roast lunch, with Barry whose birthday is on the same day as mine, opening presents before leaving.

On my birthday I had callers, cards and presents and a meal at Limetree House and Tony and Pam joined us later for coffee.

Life went on much the same, in spite of being a year older.

In April I had a very pleasant meeting up with Jack's niece Nora Armitage and husband Bobby who were now living in a very "top of the market" barn conversion after selling their former farmhouse. They had made a truly splendid home out of large buildings part of the original farmyard of Victorian vintage.

I had met Robin Liddell of Sheriff Hutton at the Bugthorpe Show in the autumn and got chatting about old farm customs. This ended with my being invited to talk to the Sheriff Hutton Social Club on "Farm Lads of the East Riding".

I was collected by Nora, and had a very pleasant tea with she and Bobby before going to the village hall.

There was a record number of members present and they proved an enthusiastic audience. I later recorded I'd sold 10 "Jack" books, and received a bouquet which was a pleasant surprise.

That month, I also had a pleasant meeting when Tim and Mary Norman from St Martins in the Scilly Isles who came for coffee one morning. They were friends through my writing in the Dalesman and bought a copy of the "Jack" book by post. I said when sending it off that I hadn't had any sales before to the Isles of Scilly!

Mary Norman later phoned, and asked if I'd been to Filey Convent as I'd mentioned a convent education. I said my daughter Maureen had been to Filey and so had Mary Norman! She was coming to Yorkshire for a Re-union, so perhaps we could meet?

Maureen had, in recent years, started meeting up with old Filey Convent girls, but hadn't been able to get to the Re-unions.

However, when Tim and Mary came that fine spring morning, we had lots to talk about and I asked Elizabeth Hodgson to call, as she had been for coffee to their lovely house (through me) when on holiday in St Martins.

Another incident of happy meetings through my modest writings.

We collected the last pack of "Jack" books from Winston Halstead, and Pam took some next day to Skidby Mill as they'd sold the first lot.

I went in May on another good canal holiday with Elizabeth Brumfield – in the midlands and ended near Oxford – described fully elsewhere.

The rather officious manner of the boat owner worried Elizabeth and Mary a lot. Emma, his wife was lovely, hard working and a good cook.

I enjoyed the company of an American couple Ruth and Neil and kept in touch – and as I write have heard they have booked with same people (but new boat) for September 2006, so they were not put off and it didn't worry me! Though naturally one expects more consideration for paying passengers

I kept calling on Eileen and one Monday Nancie drove Eileen and me to have lunch with Maureen, lovely food as usual; we had coffee in the garden and a drive to the cliff top where I stayed with Eileen to look at the views – all blue sea towards Scarborough. We stayed long enough for tea and cake with Barry coming home before we left.

In the evening we had another happy outing, at least for Nancie, myself and W.I. members to George Smith, and his famous garden in Heslington. Jennifer and I had quite a chat to George as he always makes a great fuss of us after the "Open Garden" supper at Jennifer's, which he enjoyed so much.

Ken came to lunch that fine week too, and we went up to Cot Nab and also looked at the building going on at Skirpenbeck. Ken always came laden with produce from his garden, though now walking with two sticks.

That was also a sad week as the dear Kathleen Corkery, neighbour and close friend of Jennifer had died after a long "battle" against cancer. Jennifer offered to help Dennis by having five Irish guests to stay over the Sunday funeral.

Pam, Tony and I had been invited to a big "Hog Roast" party at Towthorpe that day, so a problem of having to be in two places at once! We went to Towthorpe for drinks and nibbles and enjoyed seeing various members of the family, some we see more than others. We had to leave to go to the funeral, where the church as full and a long service as a Mass.

We went back to Towthorpe, but missed the best part of the Hog Roast, and stayed till 7 p.m. in good weather in the garden with a small marquee. About 70 guests of all ages, and Mark took a "Convenience" Loo, as in the early stages of being very much involved in them as a diversification, with farm prices falling.

Later in June too, we had the village "Open Day" with decorated wheelie bins! I'd thought this a crazy suggestion, but felt obliged to try. Fiona (opposite) kindly hosed out my bin when doing hers, and as the theme for the competition was "T.V. or film", I chose to do "Changing Rooms" a popular weekly programme at that time!

I 'papered' my bin and put decorating materials all round. Jennifer made a good attempt with "The Jungle Book" having lots of zoo soft toys and plenty of greenery. It was amazing what original ideas were thought up and displayed all over the village.

Wheelie bins became cars, tractors (we didn't think of lying them horizontal) or boats.

"Bin Gardening", "Bin on Holiday" were cleverly done, and many variations to add to a general feeling of carnival spirit, with exhibitions, a band, ice cream van and, of course, refreshments.

Bill Derrick Sykes came to join in the day, also Elizabeth Brumfield, and he drove us round.

I had a visit to the Fitz's in Wales in July, going by two trains to Chester where Jim and Mary met me, and we had lunch in the Garden Centre there.

However, on the way to the motorway Jim took a wrong turning and Mary got upset, blurting out "He's not well you know, its lung cancer!" However, he did the usual driving us around country roads during the rest of my visit.

I loved the drive to the Waterfall, where I hadn't been for several years and had memories of taking our children there. We also went over to Bala, and to Welshpool for lunch and shopping in the old station, now a bargain section of "Edinburgh Wool".

Jim had failed, but was still good company and helped with washing up. I was relieved though when they told me they'd booked a taxi to take me back to Chester.

I was home before Bishop Wilton Show, and had the usual good day there, joining Jen and William's family for a picnic lunch.

In late July, another change with 'old age' affecting another dear old friend, when Tom Sloan, was brought to stay for a few days by his son Chris, with wife Liz, who had booked in at the hotel at Hawnby.

We had tea in the courtyard before they left. Tom could still manage to look after himself well. On day Jennifer and William kindly took us to lunch at the Stone Trough at Kirkham Abbey where Tom treated us, and it was fine enough to eat outside. Afterwards we had a lovely drive back via narrow lanes to Howsham.

Chris and Liz had had a good time in Hawnby and some good walks, so it all went very well, but I wondered if it would be Tom's last visit, such a kind person and always the perfect gentleman with good manners!

Monday 16th August I had another beach day, which I so loved. Twelve of us went to the beach at Cayton and took picnics. The sea was warm and calm and I had a swim.

Children were a mixture from family and Jennifer's step ones too. I always love a short sea bathe – much better than a pool, but find now the sea isn't warm enough till August.

In September the Fitz's came by taxi and had a few days here. Jim didn't seem noticeably more frail, and they walked round the village in sunshine and we went to Pocklington with Jennifer.

We had a lovely birthday party tea for Jennifer on the 2nd when she was sixty! The Foster grandchildren plus Sophie and Nicola were all so excited to lead her blindfold out to the garden to find the big presents of a sundial and stone urn.

Jennifer, of course, was thrilled and the children all so happy to be part of the surprise.

The good weather continued and the next day we had Jane with Laura, and Lucy with Hannah to lunch. After combining Tony, Pam, Mark and Lisa all called to see our 'favourite' visitors, though tired after hard work, it was the Fitz's last evening here.

The Harvest Festival passed as usual, with an effort to decorate and the tea party after it. I did my "Teddy Bear" – A.A. Milne and knew it from memory – the diary entry for the day ends with 'tired!' It's a pity most of us who rally round and help are getting on, or have got OLD!

I had prepared some meals ahead for our friends Barbara and Gaines from Georgia, U.S.A. to visit Bishop Wilton with their daughter and son-in-law. I'd also booked them in for two nights at the Fleece. However, I had the sad news that poor Gaines had been taken ill during the flight to U.K. and ended up in the Radcliffe Infirmary, as their family lived in Faringdon.

I kept in touch for news, but when well enough Gaines and Barbara returned to U.S.A. and I wasn't able to meet them. We still write, but I fear won't be able to visit each other again. Old age is often sad!

I had an interesting lunch at the Gildings one day while Professor Maurice Beresford was visiting them.

Peter Gilding (a retired priest) and wife Wendy had met many years ago when working with Maurice on the famous "Wharram Percy Dig" and continued to be part of the team.

The Gildings came to live in what was Barbara Snape's home, and have proved to be very helpful to the village in many ways.

Peter has helped out in church, and Wendy started the popular Garden Club.

I enjoyed meeting Maurice Beresford again, and he was so interested in anything to do with Towthorpe, and the Megginson connection with the ancient village.

Sadly he died in 2005 after further deterioration – very much missed, but his work will live on.

I had a wonderful little holiday before the end of October, going to Kettering by train, and being met by Mickey's Jo and Pru and driven to Warkton. It was so lovely to meet up again after a long spell. Last time Mickey came, Ali had helped to get her here, but I hadn't seen Jo and Pru for years.

We had lots to talk about, and had a happy evening, and lovely meal at Ali's house in Kettering, where Ali is a nurse and husband Paul a police officer.

I was so thrilled to at last be able to visit Granchester where Pru drove us the next day. I had been a Rupert Brooke 'fan' since schooldays when we were taught so many of the war poems. My sister Lallie had also given me a lovely early edition of Brooke poems and the handsome photo of Rupert made him even more of an idol!

We had lunch at the famous orchard and looked round the museum before going on to Cambridge where we had tea in a café, a tour round in the car and a walk to see some of the wonderful colleges, then 'home' later to Warkton for a fish and chip supper.

The next day we were driven to Wimbledon – such a long tedious journey I thought for the girls, when making frequent visits to see their Mother in Warkton, Northants.

As Jo was worried about her Tom being in hospital with a strange 'foreign' virus, Pru kindly made Mickey and me very welcome in her pleasant ground floor flat in Raynes Park, after a walk round the Wimbledon shops.

She even made herself a bed on her kitchen floor, after we'd been to Jo's married son's flat, where we met his wife Sean and Nigel. Later Pru cooked for us.

The next morning Mickey had an appointment with an osteopath as still suffering from her stiff neck and later we went to Adrienne and Peter Jackson in their Wimbledon flat – so different from my last visit to them overlooking Lake Geneva a few years before.

Mickey hadn't met Adrienne for 75 years! A great reunion and Peter pleased to join in for a very good lunch.

We had so much to talk about and photos to see (and to take) and later Pru called for Mickey and had tea and scones with us, and said goodbye.

The weather was not very kind the next day, Saturday, but Adrienne and I went to the local supermarket and after a roast beef meal we had a rest before Peter drove us round Wimbledon Common as far as Richmond Park, and passed the Tennis Club before going back to their flat, so I saw places I'd heard of over the years, and never had a chance to visit. The last time I went to Wimbledon was when staying with Mickey before the war and saw Donald Budge play!

After a lovely two days, I got a taxi on the Sunday to Kings Cross and then a quick train to York to be met by Pam. Dear Nancie had helped with Daisy.

I had so enjoyed seeing my old friends and Mickey's helpful and lovely girls!

It was nice to see village friends again – especially Eileen who kept cheerful in spite of all her aches and pains.

On Friday October 28th we had the excitement of Sarah and Dave's wedding at the Pavilion Hotel in Fulford. Maureen and Barry collected me early, and we had coffee at the Hotel, meeting up with Dave's parents George and Heather, and Lucy, Colin and Hannah.

It was an ideal arrangement for us to spend time in the hotel lounge – Alison joined us, and Sarah had her nails done by Lucy.

We had sandwiches before going up to our hotel rooms. In the Bridal Suite we watched Sarah being helped into the beautiful gown, which suited her slim figure so well.

Later we met other guests and assembled for the ceremony. Maureen looked very smart, to give her daughter away. I read a verse chosen by Sarah and it all went off very well.

They had decided to dispense with professional photographers and David bought a special camera with tripod. The three Lefley brothers, Paul who had flown back from Europe having been on a lecture tour and only just made it to York in time, Colin and even the bridegroom David all helped in a friendly informal fashion to act as photographers.

The meal was excellent, and the flower pedestal arrangements done by Jennifer and Elizabeth Hodgson looked beautiful and were cleverly moved by hotel staff from one room to another as required. Dave and Sarah had baked and iced the cake themselves.

There was time for a rest in our rooms before the evening party began with many extra guests and I came home by midnight with Jennifer and William.

As in November three years ago when William was 60, we celebrated Jennifer's 60th by again renting Dale House in Kettlewell for the weekend. November being a so-called slack month in the farming community.

There were twenty one of us this time, and all well organised ahead for food. Jennifer planned most of it, but the young mothers were good helpers.

I had a double room to myself with shower, and lots of room on three storeys for everyone.

There were six children and this time as Ian was missing. We could 'do our own thing' in families, or join up together and it all went off very happily. Jennifer, William and I went to Grassington on the morning after handing over the key. Geoff, Rebecca and Sophie were with us. The shops were fascinating, and I bought some little Christmas ornaments to sell at the Church Bazaar.

Nancie and the McCoys had looked after Daisy who was pleased to have me back.

There was a Hunt Meet here the following Saturday and we all wondered if it would be the last.

I still saw Eileen frequently and she suffered from arthritis and ulcers on legs.

We had the Christingle service here, and Barbara Cains came to help me with the decorated oranges. At that time I used the Flexi-Bus if I needed to go to Pocklington for a hair trim or B.P. test. It was quite good, but one had to phone the day before to make a request for the bus.

Geoff Scott took me to talk at the Rotary Club in Pocklington

(Yorkways) and it went very well with good questions. I little thought that within months, Geoff would have died, and Ruth would be in care with senile trouble.

As always in December I was busy with Christmas cards and getting my designs copied by Barry for the Bazaar Sale. Toffee making is another annual job, first started in the early years at Cot Nab.

Jennifer made a lot too, and also fudge. We never had any left over.

December 2004 will be remembered in the family as the year Jennifer was really ill with a chest infection, so as she said "I had to cancel Christmas". She had coped with all her large, extended family in good time as regards presents, but on Christmas Day William cooked a small chicken and Jen ate very little.

I went to Cayton with Daisy and presents, and lots of packages after an evening with Moira and Fiona.

The Metcalfe family were all there, and we had a lovely 'Festive' time after all the preparations by Maureen and Barry who also found time to visit my old school friend Joan Laughton who was lonely and poorly.

How fortunate I am to have a large and lovely family.

On New Year's Eve Maureen and Barry had the first course of their usual 'shared' village dinner party here! They brought lots of delicious nibbles all attractively served with drinks of course. They all (16) squashed in and I too enjoyed this preliminary start to New Year, but was glad to go to bed early while the guests went on to the Quarmby's for main course.

It was lovely on Jan 2nd to have Roz Hoyes and Annette for coffee with Tony too as they were all staying in a holiday complex near Malton.

Tony and Pam had moved to "The Stables" at Skirpenbeck, and glad to be in their own home again, at last!

The party in the cottage was on January 3rd 2005; I did some preparations in the previous few days. On the 3rd Jennifer came round to help me and got the spare table from the garage, heavy and needing some manipulation to fit it in the kitchen.

Lucy and Hannah got here early, twenty-two meant quite a squash, but the food lasted well. I was tired by the time helpers left, and glad to flop into bed.

Sad news on January 13th that Geoff Scott had died of cancer, which had returned. Poor Ruth not 'with it' though, and her daughters came to help.

Geoff and Ruth had been in the village since our early days at Cot Nab and taken part in all things connected with village life. I specially remember Geoff as Chairman of Parish Council when I was a member and it was a sad funeral.

A rather strange funeral was that of Angela Cottam who had been Lord Halifax's personal secretary for many years.

When we were on the Macmillan Cancer Committee, Angela was a help to me as Secretary, and always did the minutes and much of the work. She was also 'supportive' to Jennifer when she had cancer. Angela had had breast cancer which returned later. In life Angela was decidedly a none believer and had insisted there were no clergymen at her funeral and no hymns.

Jennifer took me to Octon Crematorium and it all seemed very strange. Lord and Lady Halifax both spoke very sincerely of Angela's help to them.

A happier day was at Baswick for a birthday lunch for Ken – given at Martin's house. Tony and Pam took me – all very pleasant with a ride round the farm.

Hilary Mason came to lunch and brought a copy of her family history for us to read which we all found fascinating, and I posted it round to the others to enjoy with many memories recalled.

The Rev. Derek Hodgson was in hospital after a fall in the road, and I went to see him with Elizabeth. Sadly this proved the beginning of a long illness and we missed him very much in church as he helped James such a lot, not only in taking services, but also in playing the organ, and giving amusing monologues at our concerts. Derek and Elizabeth had to cancel a long awaited Caribbean cruise.

I saw two good films in January at Pocklington Arts Centre – "Ladies in Lavender" with Judi Dench. I went with Elizabeth Brumfield after she had lunch here one day. It was an excellent film, which we really enjoyed.

Shortly after that, I went to see "Merchant of Venice" one evening with William and Jennifer. Another good film which made me long to see Venice while I'm still able to get around. We are very lucky to have the Arts Centre in Pocklington.

I was so sorry in early February to have a call from Nora Loftus-Bryan's cousin Daphne to say dear Nora had died.

I knew she had been in a catholic nursing home in Geneva after a fall and broken hip. I had felt sorry for her situation with French speaking companions, but she was cheerful in letters (never a grumbler!) and pleased if her church friends took her out.

She had asked for two packets of my church Bazaar notelets, so I'd recently posted them and, of course, never knew who used them!

James Finnemore was pleased to arrange a small service for Nora on same day as her funeral in Geneva. Friends and a few relations came to it and we felt Nora would be pleased. She had been such a devoted member of St. Edith's P.C.C. and so generous to the church. Later she left a good legacy.

Around the same time in February I had a lovely 'unknown' guest in Vicki Marshall.

Vicki is the daughter of Eric Pearce, the ex husband of Lallie. She has lived in Cornwall since returning with her parents from Australia as a teenager.

Sadly her Mother died at an early age, also her sister as a young wife with children. Eric had told me of all this on telephone calls, and I also heard from Lallie, especially after Lallie and Eric shared a home for a few years in old age.

Vicki had married, but was close to her Father, and cared for him when failing in health till he died aged 92.

Now Vicki had got in touch with me as the last person to know Eric in Yorkshire, and I'd asked her to stay while also making contact with one or two other 'Pearce' relations from family history.

Pam took me to York and we shopped before going to the station a bit late, after I had been waiting in the wrong car park!!

However, I soon recognised Vicki, a quite unfazed and attractive girl waiting near the taxi rank.

We all got on well together during her few days here – so easy in the cottage, and so pleased to meet others in the family. She had a copy of 'Eric's Life', which was quite amazing though not easy to read as the printing was poor.

Vicki had a "garden plant" business in South West Cornwall and was intrigued by all our village snowdrops, which don't grow in Cornwall, and keen to take photos.

Jennifer took her to Givendale to show her more, and Pam took Vicki and me out for a day in the Hull area.

We three enjoyed this day, of exploring places connected with Eric's family, I was specially pleased to show her the Pearce bungalow in Newland Park, opposite my childhood home and from which Lallie and Eric were married.

Eric's father had been an Estate Agent with an office in the 'Old Town', and we found the street, so Vicki could take photos. Our day out included the Humber Bridge (so cold and windy I stayed in the car) and having lunch in the shopping precinct of what was, in my day, the Dock area

– now "Princes' Quay".

We had lots to talk about, while Vicki was here and photographs to look at.

A cousin on the Pearce side collected Vicki here on the Sunday and she stayed two days in York before going back to her husband and her plant nursery in Cornwall.

Soon after that Eileen was rushed into hospital for an emergency hernia operation, but got over it quite well, and the Rev. Derek Hodgson came home after a month in hospital, but was never himself again and could no longer take services, play the organ or enjoy his crosswords, intensive reading or using his piano for pleasure.

William was mentioned in my diary as being 'busy with Father' one snowy Sunday morning, and for many months Charlie Foster had ill health, memory loss at times and visits to hospital with a cancerous tumour on his head.

A distressing time for Mary and the family, and William was a devoted and caring son.

In spite of snow Jim and Mary Fitzpatrick came here by taxi on February 21st. I had little hope of them setting off from Wales, but so pleased to see them safely here, having had no trouble on the roads.

The driver didn't stay long and we had a fishcake lunch, a fireside afternoon with Jennifer calling with Libby (dog) and took Daisy out for me.

The next day, still snowy, Jennifer and William had an appointment, but dropped us off at Jane's in Bolton for coffee, where it was nice to see her and the children. Later we had lunch at the Gold Cup in Catton and Maureen called after work.

The next day my guests were entertained with Nancie here too for coffee and James joining us for lunch.

Later Pam took us to Skirpenbeck – Tony was delayed after pulling out a motorist stuck in snow on Givendale road.

After a good 'Dining room' meal we were driven home in blizzard conditions!

We were all concerned about the return taxi drive to Wales next day, but the driver had been in York overnight and they set off without delay at 1.30 p.m. – and no trouble. Lovely to have had them here, Jim failing in health and strength, but still able to enjoy everything. Maureen came as usual for supper, bed and breakfast.

It was good to have Eileen back home, and I visited her with Daisy.

I also stayed with Derek Hodgson sometimes as Elizabeth worried about leaving him. He still liked to keep going out for little walks and 'fresh air'. It seemed rather an odd situation, that 'poor old Irene' was his minder! I helped out in this way a few times over the next weeks. Derek continued to deteriorate, but could be left safely most of the time.

William's father was having more trouble with head skin cancer, and had another operation. He needed a lot of help over the months.

There were the usual birthday celebrations in the family, as March to May include several. I went out with Maureen for the day on my birthday, lunch at the Balloon Tree where Matthew Machin gave us complimentary ice cream sundaes as a present. After that we looked round the McArthur Glen Designer Outlet near Fulford (up William's "Golden Road") and made a few purchases. I was pleased with a cream cotton bedspread for the spare room. The "Golden Road" is so called by the family, as the Fosters owned the field where an access road was needed!

Nancie and I did the sorting out and saw to the distribution of the church magazine called the "Parish Pump" every two months, and I pushed them through the 'top end' of village street. I felt it more worthwhile when the magazine contained general as well as church news, as one felt more people really read it!

Poor Daisy got an awful bash on her thigh when I swung the heavy chancel gate as she was going through when in church for a cleaning session!

I had to get Lily Jebson to go for her car to get the poor dog home. Jennifer came round to see her, and we decided nothing broken and a little aspirin with lots of tender loving care was all we could do.

I was worried for my dear old dog, but she didn't lose her appetite, and very gradually improved, but slept downstairs for a time, until obviously wanting to come up to her bed in my room, so I resorted to carrying her. It was easier going down!

She was very lame for a few weeks, but eventually completely 'sound' again.

In mid April for Pam's birthday present I decided to celebrate with a day flight for the two of us (having found she was in favour) to Venice from Yeadon Airport.

After seeing the film of "Merchant of Venice" at the Pocklington Arts Centre and shots of Venice it made me long to see it while still fit enough to go.

We had to get up about 4 a.m. and make the journey to the airport to check in at the scheduled time. We sat over coffee in the lounge and found a great number of passengers booked for this comparatively short flight.

The breakfast was adequate – good sausages I remember – and on arrival in Venice we had quite a long quick walk (for me at 86) and a wait on a landing stage for the boat booked to take us across the lagoon. By mistake, not enough room for a joint venture with a party from Exeter! The rain poured down as we 'sailed' across and though a good commentary visibility was poor.

We were soon amazed by the wonderful city as we walked over little bridges to St. Mark's Square. Here the rain came in torrents with thunder and lightening. Some of our party bought cagoules from a vendor in the square. We managed with umbrellas – and all sheltered under the colonnades for a lecture from a guide.

Luckily the rain stopped as we came out from a short tour of the factory where we saw glass blowing, and an exhibition of the famous, but costly Venetian glass.

We ate ice creams in St Mark's Square, and we walked around taking in the unique beauty of this city, even more impressive than we imagined.

I loved the little canals, the gondolas, the colour of ancient houses with foundations in water, and the exotic mosaics and grandeur of the famous buildings and churches.

The sun was quite hot, so I took off my jacket and sat to watch the mass of activity around the lagoon landing places. I'd suggested that Pam had an hour or so, on her own to go at her quicker pace, to explore streets and shops.

After that, we had booked a tour on the motorboat for the Grand Canal rather than the shorter one on a gondola and felt we saw more that way.

Another stop near the square for coffee brought out by smart waiters, and we were even given a share of gigantic ice-creams offered by neighbouring ladies from Yorkshire who found they couldn't manage all the ones they'd ordered.

After another walk round exotic shops, and the outside of the cathedral (too late for entry by then) we walked back to our boat. This crossing was better with good views. There seemed unnecessary delay over boarding cards at the airport and the return so called 'dinner' was boring (more sausages) but the day had been a great joy to both of us. I kept awake till Pam left me at my door at 11.30 p.m.!

Also in April 2006 we read of the death of Colin Newlove after hearing rumours. This was a shock, as he had phoned me a short time before to tell me he'd had a successful operation for knee replacement. Colin had been important in our lives since early Cot Nab years. What fun we had with horses, badgers (pet ones!) and the bulls he rode!

I wrote to Helen, but Jennifer and I were booked to go on an F.W.C. outing to Rennishaw Hall in Derbyshire that day of the funeral. I phoned Helen afterwards and with Jennifer we spent an evening at Selley Bridge having a good long talk with Helen and daughter Nicola who was still at home.

Colin had been part of our lives for so long, and a great character, written of in my books in detail. He'd died quickly after a blood clot followed his apparently successful operation and his age was kept secret as he wished!

I also had my birthday treat at the end of April. I'd requested "A day in the Lake District" from William and Jennifer and eventually found a suitable date on April 29th.

It was a memorable day in good weather and William chose a good drive round Ullswater on our way to Windermere, to start the boat trip to Bowness. I thoroughly enjoyed it, and the expensive, but exclusive "bar meal" sitting in the window at the Old England Hotel! Another request, which I'd longed to do since childhood holidays when lunch at such a grand hotel would have been out of all question.

I thought a lot, during that day, of those holidays with Pam, and her family. Great memories! That was indeed, a very special birthday treat!

Jennifer had her family Christmas Day in May as she missed giving one when so ill in December.

We had a wonderful midday meal with two tables and excellent catering for 21.

Martin Layzell had chosen that day to bring his father, Roy to visit Tony, so they picked me up at Limetree House, meeting Jen and William briefly as the family were leaving. I joined in a drive round Wold villages with Tony in his 'best' Range Rover before having tea at the Stables. So another special day.

After the Village Hall Fayre – an annual event, I went with Elizabeth Brumfield to have lunch at the theatre in Scarborough before seeing a play, which we found somewhat incomprehensible! Elizabeth had tea and cake here.

I had a few days with Jim and Mary in Wales after that, having no trouble with trains and met at Chester by the Welsh taxi driver they kindly arranged for me.

Jim had failed in health by then, but was still driving and good company. We had some lovely drives and one to Welshpool where I always enjoy shopping in the old station complex. I bought a beach-bag for Jane's birthday and a shirt and cardigan for myself. We had a good lunch there too.

We also went to Bala, and Anne came over for lunch – and I spoke to John on the phone.

It was lovely to have time to just sit and talk, and to look out at the view of the river alongside the garden, and I had no trouble getting home.

Soon after that holiday we went to Sally's wedding in a Harrogate hotel. William and Jennifer had to find space in the car for flowers and pedestal, as once more Jennifer was doing the floral arrangements. After getting the flowers fixed in place, we met others in both families, had photos taken and coffee in the lounge.

Nicola looked like a very elegant fashion model, walking so gracefully and certainly more than her fourteen years! Sophie looked sweet in her long dress and pretty hairstyle.

Sally made a beautiful bride, and looked so happy with Jeff for the ceremony. I read two verses they had chosen and the weather was warm enough for photographs in the hotel garden.

We had a happy table for lunch and afterwards I went to my room for a rest. Some of the family went shopping, but the weather changed to rain.

In the evening there was a lively disco, and buffet meal for over a hundred friends and relations before going up to our bedrooms. This was a first wedding for Jeff and we felt happy for him.

It was fun finding others in the family, all meeting for breakfast on the Sunday morning, before Jennifer and William took me to see Coidy who was in Harrogate nursing home 'Larchfield' for her annual visit to Yorkshire. I had lunch with her and caught up with family news and heard all about other Yorkshire friends who visited her. Later Maureen and Barry came to collect me as they were by then, at the party for Hannah's second birthday.

Coidy at 95 was still sprightly, smart and an entertaining speaker, but more deaf and having difficulty with short sight.

Lucy and Colin had to abandon the idea of a garden party with B.B.Q. as a thunderstorm put a stop to outdoor fun for little friends, and their parents, but all went off well indoors.

Life continued in the village with visits to poor Eileen who was gradually having even more aches and pains as well as trouble with the ulcers on legs and infected toes. There were always little jobs to be done in garden, courtyard and cottage, letters to write and books to read, to say nothing of "Neighbours" my only soap on T.V. and other distractions.

Jennifer and William were away for their annual three weeks with caravan in France and Mary Foster coping with William's father who had increasing difficulties with his skin cancer, and old age problems at 98.

That year 2005 will always be remembered for the Royal Ascot at York. We enjoyed reading all about it, and watching our televisions. The Queen and the Duke stayed at Garrowby, going daily to Bishopthorpe Palace for lunches before the Royal Drive to the racecourse with horses, carriages and all the usual pomp and ceremony, a delight to watch.

Maureen and Barry asked Daisy and me to stay at Cayton for a weekend in June and I had a lovely relaxing time in HOT weather. We had a meal out at a fish restaurant in East Ayton, with a glorious drive round all my favourite places on the Sunday and a picnic by the river in Brompton. Later we sat out in the garden and in the evening went to Filey – a really lovely day.

On the Monday, after I helped Maureen in the kitchen, she drove to Scarborough where we enjoyed charity shops and the 'Posh' nearly new one. We called on my old school friend Joan Laughton who is lonely but in better health, before returning to get a meal ready for Jennifer and William. Jennifer had returned from France very lame after falling over the caravan step at the end of the holiday. We had a good meal, a walk down to beach (Jen and I sat while others walked) and they brought Daisy and I home by 10 o'clock. My back porch was flooded as the door had blown open and I bruised my leg badly when flinging the sodden mat outside!

Michelle, Jennifer's adopted daughter, had another degree at Bishop Burton College and we (Jennifer and I) were invited to the ceremony in a huge HOT marquee – Jennifer still lame! Derek and Sue Rivis were also there – we all had tea afterwards, and photos taken in the very hot studio.

On Lisa's 30th birthday, I went up to Cot Nab in wonderful sunshine for a barbeque lunch with Pam, Tony, Ian, Jane, Edward and Laura. Also Lisa's friend and young son. They erected Mark's small marquee on the old tennis court (half the original size) and I helped clean the old summerhouse, which we had loved, and Tony and Pam had ignored! I was pleased to think it would be used again, and at night they had a big party and hog roast.

Ian took me down to the village where I joined in, and judged, Ann Sumpner's Ascot Hat party in aid of the village hall, but not many there on a perfect evening for sitting out in the garden.

Another hot evening at Kirby Underdale Strawberry Supper at the vicarage, and one day my diary says "too hot to be in courtyard".

Ian went off to work in Cambridgeshire where he would share a cottage and do his 'year out' for a huge farming company, "Greens of Soham". We had a meal at Millington before he left with all family there.

Because of Tom Sloan's deteriorating health we decided to meet at Saltaire Mill. Tony drove me, and Chris took Tom who needed a wheelchair. Sad to see him so bad on his legs and weak in voice, but we all enjoyed the day. A lunch and so much to see apart from Hockney's pictures. Interesting history of Saltaire too. Tony chose a watercolour print of the Wolds by Hockney £60, but no money so I provided it, and said it could be their Christmas present! We were sad to say goodbye to the Sloans, but had a good drive in rain!

Then came the annual family picnic on July 12th. I went to church with William and Jennifer – their 'Disco' packed high with food, barbeque etc. We arrived at our Levisham wayside field by 12.30 and found many of the family already there – very good weather and the various 'gazebos' used for shade from sun, rather than to shelter from rain, as had happened some years.

I went round the assortment of food offered, both hot and cold, stopping to sit down to eat, though my appetite is always small nowadays.

The children were in their element, rushing down through trees to the stream in wellies, and returning with wet clothes, but smiling faces. Some of the Dads seemed to enjoy acting as lifeguards too! We had the usual walk to the station and steam trains, and arrived home about 7 o'clock to walk Daisy, while still warm enough to sit out in courtyard. Nancie had kindly seen to Daisy during the day.

The Raymonds from Devon arrived at Tony and Pam's during the following week. I was so pleased to see them again, but sorry, like us, to be getting older. Rose had a difficult bladder problem too, but coped well.

The weather was still perfect. Tony and Pam took them for a long drive to the Dales one day, and another time lent the car for Dick to drive Rose and me to the coast, and we had a meal at the café on Oliver's Mount. We also went to the open garden at Thixendale where the Braders have an especially good garden with a lot of variety. So hot and many people there.

In the evening after our Scarborough drive, I did a meal here and Jennifer and William brought wine and cheeses.

Our Bishop Wilton Show Day went well, as usual with kind weather, and the next day Pam took Elizabeth and me to meet our bus as start of the Irish Cruise. I have written a full account of this very enjoyable holiday, so enough to say it was a good ship, the Black Prince and good company. I loved what we saw of Ireland too and had an afternoon on Tresco in the Isles of Scilly and met up with Tim and Mary from St. Martins.

Charlie Foster had a quiet lunch at home with family for his 99th birthday. I had Nicola for the day, as she was staying in Bishop Wilton with Jennifer and William.

Charlie had been in failing health for months, with William being very much involved in helping to look after him. Hospital visits when Jennifer often went too.

On August 5th I went to Scarborough with Daisy to join the family holiday in a tall, Victorian terrace house on Esplanade road.

It was an ideal house for the children (Thomas, Jack, Cameron, Sophie and Nicola permanently with others to join during the week) and very well equipped.

The weather was uncertain on some days, but we managed to visit other beaches. The men, Jon and Geoff were wonderful helpers. Simon came for one night and William took the caravan to Cayton with the dogs to be near some of the time. We had visits from Maureen, Barry, Tony and Pam, plus Pam one day with Jane and children.

Richard, Ann-Marie and children were there on the Sunday. Sometimes I opted out of the 'group' with Daisy, one day I visited my old school friend, Joan Laughton, in her flat in Westbourne Grove.

Jennifer and I shared a two-bedded room at the top of the house, and getting Daisy up the twisting staircase wasn't easy. Jennifer carried her up for me, but going down was simple as long as I kept her from going too fast. I often had her on a lead in the house and tied her up if our outings were not suitable. I paid £20 extra to take my dog! (Not even a sheet or towel provided!)

I thoroughly enjoyed my seaside holiday, but think Daisy was pleased to be back at home. I only had one swim and that was in the pool on the North side. We had an afternoon in Peasholm Park and I found the 'Battleship' displays had changed very little since pre-war visits from Hull, and later ones with our children. We went to the little circus one evening and saw the wall of death that reminded me of Hull Fair evenings in school days and with Jack. This time the bikes – 3 of them were ridden up, down and around a steel globe of criss-cross design for the audience to see through. Quite amazing, noisy and thrilling to watch. I wished Jack could have seen it.

I still enjoyed the Farm Women's Club monthly meetings, and in August had a visit to the walled garden at Helmsley with Clare Potts, and her husband. We stopped briefly on the way at Kirkham Abbey, and were lucky to see the Flying Scotsman pass through on one of the 'steam trips' from York to Scarborough. I also got Jennifer's birthday presents (aprons!) in Helmsley.

My dear friend Eileen Hopper had had her 90th birthday on August 6th when I was away, so Nancie and I gave her a treat on the 18th. A sunny day with Eileen enjoying the countryside she knows well. We called on Nancie's daughter who drove us all around Scarborough, and up to Oliver's Mount café for tea.

Nancie drove us home via Forge Valley; I don't think we could have given Eileen a better treat.

There was a wedding in St. Edith's on a Sunday for Debbie Sefton and I was the only person available to ring the bells! I told James I had retired from that job, but no good "just give them a tingling" he said. So I put on a nice dress, sat at the back of a church full of smart guests and at the end of the service, managed to give short bursts of a peal with little breaks to recover my breath!

Debbie was a pretty bride, and her mother Ruth was so grateful for my services – not only the official fee of £10, but also a nice card, photograph and an especially good talcum powder as a present! I'd had stiff neck trouble beforehand, but it didn't make it any worse.

The last weekend in August was our Flower Festival in aid of Church and Village Hall, what a lot of work and preparation. On the Thursday afternoon I helped with refreshments for the poor, harassed flower club members who seemed to be making a lot of mess to clear up while creating the most beautiful and ingenious arrangements, with hard working Jean Singleton as their leader.

Elizabeth Hodgson and Jennifer did one depicting our W.I. The whole theme was Bishop Wilton activities.

The preview on the Friday evening was a big success. Mark had taken his white marquee to the churchyard near the rear door and our W.I. catering committee produced wonderful small savouries. Eighty guests, so all worthwhile. I read A.A. Milne's "Geraniums red and Delphiniums blue".

Over the weekend, I took turns as steward in church and saw a lot of people I knew, including Peter and Joan Atkinson. Bobby and Nora Armitage called on their way home on Sunday evening and we sat in the courtyard.

The refreshments at the Rectory were very good with stalls too. The exhibition of village life in the village hall was well attended.

By the end of the weekend we all felt tired, but relieved it had been a great success. Nancie had done so much on the organising and secretarial side. James' parents were staying with him and were also a great help.

Two thousand five hundred pounds raised for the church, £5000 altogether. Nancie had had a lot of work in getting sponsors in the early stages to raise the money needed for the flower club expenses.

My duty as church cleaner the next week with Jill Dixon-Carter was a harder job than usual.

I had a lovely day out with Jane Megginson on a sunny September day. Farndale and lunch at the little pub there, then up to Danby and over to Rosedale for tea and cake.

Glorious views on top of 'the bank' and home via Jane's mother's villages before her marriage to Uncle Edward.

Harvest progressed with stops for rain or breakdown of machinery, one night Tony had been working through till morning to beat the weather and finish combining.

Ian was working in the Fen country near Soham with a large firm called "Green's" who supplied many acres of beetroot to supermarkets and other root crops, corn and daffodils. They also had land in neighbouring Norfolk, Suffolk and Essex, so he was seeing a lot of different countryside. He shared a cottage and was happy in the work.

September 24th was quite a full day as I went to Connie Beaulah's memorial service in Givendale Church. Lady Holderness and Emma were there. Elizabeth Brumfield and I went on to the buffet lunch at the Feathers. It was nice to meet all the Beaulah family again from Cot Nab period.

After that I went with Elizabeth to Seaton Ross to sit out in the sun and to have tea, and later to a choir concert in the church with supper! Churchwarden Keith kindly brought me home at 11pm., to find Jennifer wondering where I'd been, and she had news that Sarah and David had a baby boy Samuel, born three weeks early!

Jennifer, Maureen and I went to see Mother and baby in York hospital on the Monday, after lunch at Dean's nursery and all was well.

Harvest festivals followed and the usual hectic work of decorating and providing food for the Sunday evening supper in Bishop Wilton. Elizabeth Hodgson was poorly and no one extra to help with the decorating and Lily valiantly did the two pedestals.

The tea party evening went well, and the school children with James did Widdecombe Fair. I made a long hobbyhorse by fixing a head on a clothes prop! I read Stanley Holloway's "football match". All went well to our relief.

Early in October poor Eileen was whisked into hospital – so much pain with leg ulcers and her heart was causing problems.

I went to see her once a week on the "Medi-Bus" which was also used by her sister-in-law Helen. Eileen had very few relations. I found Eileen rather depressed and my visits were short because of the Medi-Bus times. One afternoon Jennifer took me after we had been to the Garden Centre (Deans) and after calling on Dave, Sarah and Samuel, we thought Eileen was looking better, but the ward was a dismal place with no one really able to hold a conversation.

During Eileen's period in hospital we had the real pleasure of a visit from the Ballards! We'd tried to get them organised to come, all the summer, but not easy as Mickey had to be driven by Pru and Jo, and difficult when all were free at the same time.

However, they eventually arrived on Sunday October 16th, rather late as delayed by fog in Northants. Tony and Pam called in the afternoon to see them. It was lovely to see them, and we had a cold meal with a hot one in the evening. Jennifer came round to take Jo and Pru to Limetree as more bedroom and bathroom space than here.

The next day – Monday – Jennifer drove us all to Scarborough, Forge Valley, Langdale, Troutsdale and Dalby Forest where we at last found somewhere to eat! The shop there was good and we bought things, and at Thornton Dale Jo even found a wedding outfit!

The Ballards were very taken with Yorkshire scenery and lack of traffic. They kept saying, "We must come more often". They (the girls) hadn't been in Yorkshire together since school holidays at Cot Nab where they remembered so much fun with Jack.

We ended that day with a lovely meal with Tony and Pam at the Stables, which they were pleased to see, and we had a lot of laughs.

On Tuesday Pru drove us to Bainton where we ate and shopped at "Wold Village" before calling on Maureen in Pocklington, and found charity shop bargains in the town. That evening we had a good meal with Jennifer and William – so I got off lightly with cooking.

The next day, I packed a picnic lunch, and sadly said "Goodbye" to our visitors. I was surprised and pleased by how much 'the girls' remembered of their farm holidays as children. They loved looking at my old photos and recognised 'Jess' Jack's old toy horse who stands on the landing here.

That week I had the great pleasure of a clear sunny early evening flight in Nigel Rudsdale's plane. He had tried some time before, but as visibility was poor we only circled the villages. This time, with wonderful sky and visibility, Nigel flew over the Humber, parts of Hull and along the coast I knew so well. He even circled over Fraisthorpe twice and on the way back we saw a lot of Sledmere, Cot Nab, and so to Full Sutton airfield.

We had a special treat driving back to Bishop Wilton when a Barn Owl flew slowly along at hedge top level from Youlthorpe, resting on a low post for us to have a better view before we left him in a tree!

I had a visit from Lucy and Sarah with Hannah and Samuel, and another day went with Jennifer, Rebecca, Geoff and Sophie to have lunch with Sally. I am so lucky to have so many of the family within easy visiting distance. Another day I had a Sunday roast dinner at Jennifer's with Kate and Cameron there.

I always enjoyed the Limetree 'roasts' as have never cooked one for myself since Jack died.

As the dark evenings meant coal or wood fires, I did more writing of this book and knitted scarves in "Funky Wool" as fashionable things to sell on my church bazaar stall.

My neighbours Isobel and John McCoy were packed up to move to the other end of the village as another baby nearly due and Sydney now three. John Sleightholme had bought their house to let it.

Dear Eileen died on November 10th after only one day in bed all the time. James was there with Helen and another relation, Kathleen, during the day, but she died in late evening before James could get to the hospital from a show meeting. He had been so good to Eileen and no one could have given a greater service to the church over a lifetime than Eileen had done.

I always enjoyed my morning visits to her, after the shop with Daisy. Eileen loved Daisy and in Witton House years had looked after her if I was out for a day.

Eileen and I enjoyed reading the same sort of books, and we always had a lot to talk about. She kept her cottage (rented from the Estate at no cost) it must have been one of the last of Lord Halifax's employees' cottages to be left to the widow, and in this case Eileen was still permitted to live there with a second husband. Sadly both husbands died of Cancer, and she had no children.

Before the funeral there was the Kirby Underdale dinner in their village hall. Always a popular affair and this time the theme was the Second World War.

I had found a Jaeger dress in black velvet, which was beautifully made – (charity shop bargain) and I added a red belt and scarf. Also a band in my hair with poppy. There were some good costumes. Maureen and Barry came to go with me and they looked very much 1940's. A very good evening.

Eileen would have been so surprised to have such a full church for her funeral. I went to the morning communion first with a few close friends with the coffin already in church. James spoke so well of Eileen's work for the church and her title of "The Boss" among the P.C.C.

I couldn't stay for the 'party' afterwards at the pub, as had to meet Elizabeth Brumfield at "The Feathers" in Pocklington. Margaret our cruise friend was visiting a Yorkshire friend and wanted to meet us again. They came here for coffee and cake after the lunch.

I missed Eileen in her house by the church and our conversations. I expect Daisy missed her too.

I had done a painting of an imagined snow scene for a Christmas card and asked Mike Pratt about getting it printed. He was most helpful and through E-Bay (?) found a quite cheap method on photographic paper – so I ordered fifty.

I then had to cut red card to stick them on, and white folded paper as a lining, so it all proved quite laborious! However, in due course they were appreciated.

Barry printed out notelets from my three designs and they were better than last year for the church bazaar.

One Sunday Sue Cartledge collected me to go for a meal (November 21st) at Skirpenbeck. We found Tony lying on the floor, and occasionally crawling round the house. He spent most of the following week in his bed! The Cartledge children were a great joy to Tony and Pam.

Charlie Foster died on November 25th so William and Jennifer had a lot to do. William had been at Birks to sleep for two nights, so was there when Charlie died in his sleep. Mary was wonderfully strong, as one would expect. Charlie was nearly 100, Mary 95, and they had had a long marriage and never moved from the house they went to after the honeymoon!

On a very cold day, November 30th, Pam and I attended the inauguration ceremony for the new Archbishop of York. Pam representing Kirby Underdale Church and myself Bishop Wilton.

There were crowds round the Minster and John Sentamu being the first black Archbishop was certainly different, and made the journey from Bishopthorpe by boat, walking from the landing stage.

We were directed to our seats in the Minster after showing our cards and had a pleasant surprise when John Megginson (Fimber Church) was in the same row, so we could sit with him.

I expected a rather tedious wait till ceremonies began, but with so much going on, and with John to talk to, the time passed very quickly. Several processions formed in varying aisles, and 'high up' clergy in wonderfully ornate robes were stationed near the great door (well within our sight) waiting for the Archbishop to arrive. Great cheers of welcome from the crowds outside in very cold temperatures.

We saw little of Sentamu, other than his colourful mitre, as he isn't very tall, but the whole service was bright, light, and yet very meaningful with wonderful choirs and the surprising addition of chanting African dancers.

We could follow the sermon on the T.V. screens, and it was all most impressive with the 'washing of feet' with school children taking part.

At the end, with the new Archbishop proceeding to St. Michael's church midst a cloud of balloons on which was written a Christian message, we queued for our picnic food! Wine or fruit juice, and a carrier bag (M&S) containing a vegetable flap, fruit (apple or banana) and a packet of crisps and crunchy bar. The organisation was amazingly perfect.

Later I went down the nave to get near the bare-chested dancers, still singing, and the women in costumes. I was quite intrigued by it all. Pam had a heavy cold and didn't want to be too close to the crowds. It was a wonderful day and a privilege to be part of such an important occasion.

On December 2nd, Maureen and I went to Charlie's funeral in Bossall church. A nice day, to be greeted in the porch by William and Jennifer. The church was full of course, as Charlie had led a life of farming that had seen many changes in agriculture. He had travelled too, and held important offices in the Potato Marketing Board. There were many old friends, and an excellent address by the Revd. Jeremy Valentine. William's sister Ruth gave a very good eulogy, in a calm, controlled and sincere manner.

After the funeral service, Birks Farm was overflowing with guests – good food, and as at a lot of funerals happy meetings of old friends and relations.

Mary coped well once more, and sat in the far sitting room in front of a roaring fire to receive guests, making them all feel welcome.

In the evening, I went to the 'school' fund raising party at Fiona Quarmby's so was very tired and late to bed – thinking of another busy day to follow – the Saturday morning Church Bazaar!

However, all went well, Peggy and I sold most of our goods on the stall, helped by some of Eileen's bits and pieces. I had the usual lunch party afterwards.

On the Monday, the W.I. Christmas Evening with games and supper was very pleasant. It's worth noting that Dorothy Flint, brought from Pocklington, enjoyed herself at 99 years!

That week started with a worry about not catching the mouse of which I'd found many traces in the cupboard under the sink, and had had the annoying job of moving drawers after scrubbing them out, and throwing 'contaminated' goods in the bin.

On December 8th, I record at the top of diary "caught mouse" and over the next week or two added six more. Such a relief after having to keep emptying drawers and cupboards. They'd been nibbling even paper while running around.

The rest of December followed the usual pattern of getting cards written and I was pleased with the ones from my painting, which Mike Pratt got copied on photographic paper at a more reasonable charge.

At Skirpenbeck Carol service, where I went with Nancie and Lily, it was a very moving end to find Mary on a donkey at the back of the church.

I got the decorations in the cottage done without trouble and pleased that the tree lights actually worked.

On December 21st I went carol singing!! James asked if I'd join the group going to Garrowby and I could ring bells! My singing is so bad I never do more than whisper.

Actually it proved to be quite a memorable evening – carrying torches and the odd instrument. Peter Gilding (retired priest) was with us too, and besides 'Garrowby Lodge' houses, we went to Home Farm and the houses there and other bungalows in the pitch-dark roads around the park.

We ended in the back hall at Garrowby with very strong drink! I had to have more ginger bread to counteract the effect. Altogether most enjoyable – Lord and Lady H. were in good form and made us very welcome.

Jennifer and I paid our usual Christmas call on Michelle (Jennifer's adopted daughter) and Darryl and found their room quite crowded with extra friends there. We always meet up a few times a year.

On Christmas Eve, Ian, Mark and Lisa called with gifts, then to Fiona's usual drinks party with Maureen and Barry before Midnight Mass.

On Christmas morning we found the shower leaking in the sitting room! We exercised Daisy, made rum sauce – called on Jennifer and William before driving to Lucy and Colin's for good present opening with Hannah exited. Excellent Turkey meal, and Barry's sticky toffee pud, extra good!

We got home 6.30 p.m. and Barry and Mo left. I phoned Tony about bathroom leak.

A very happy Boxing Day with Jennifer and William at Rebecca's with their friends too.

On December 27th we had some snow and I was doubtful about Elizabeth Brumfield driving over for a simple fishcake meal. Tony and Pam called in working clothes and Tony sorted out the shower problem and in spite of a little more snow Elizabeth got home safely in daylight.

Maureen's boss Maggie had sent me the 'Singing Westie' toy dogs on Christmas Eve after they'd amused clients in the shop. They proved a great novelty to all my visitors as well as children! I grew quite fond of them myself as long as they didn't perform too often.

On December 28th I went to Cot Nab for lunch with Lisa's Grannie from Hull and had a very pleasant time. Curly, Jane and children were there for a short spell of sledging in thawing snow. They got rather wet and cold.

The next day was Maureen and Barry's party at Cayton, and I went with Tony and Pam. We met Des, Alison's partner, and lovely to see all Mo's family. Ian was with us, and fifteen altogether with excellent catering as usual.

There was more snow to end the year, but Tony, Pam and I were lucky to get to the Stone Trough on December 30th as Martin Layzell and most of their family were spending New Year near Malton. We had a lovely, lively time – more like a private party, and fifteen present, a surprise to us to find it was Roy's 85th birthday with a cake too. We got home 11.30.

We had four Layzells to call here next afternoon and Jen joined us with William. So 2005 ended with Maureen and Barry coming for the usual Bishop Wilton New Year party which lasted till 3.30 a.m. and they stayed overnight.

I am happy to look back on it, feeling grateful for my lovely family and good health considering my age.

2006

New Year 2006 started with the worry of dear old Daisy becoming incontinent – she was very deaf and had been for some time, and eyes were looking as if cataracts forming, but she was still lively and able to go upstairs each night. However, she was 15 and I've always faced up to having to let dogs go, before getting very miserable with old age, and weeing in this cottage was a big problem with carpets everywhere and rugs in kitchen.

January 2nd was my planned family party, so Jennifer kindly took Daisy where there was a brick floor in porch and where she could be let out in the garden. Jennifer also helped a lot with the party preparations, with less people as other arrangements previously made by some.

Less of a crowd, meant it was easier to find seats for all, Sarah and Samuel were the first to arrive at 3 p.m. – I can quite understand that some of the husbands would rather find excuses to be busy!!

All went well, and food in plenty, with those with families leaving earlier, and later ones, Tony, Pam, William and Jennifer helping to clear up by 9.30. By then I felt tired.

The next day Jennifer and I took dear Daisy to the vet in Pocklington to be put to sleep. It was such an easy death. Stroking her till she collapsed on the table. I said to the vet "Oh Angus, I wish I could come to you if things get difficult for me to carry on with my life!" I feel strongly that, so many people have to live far longer than they'd wish with immobility and deterioration of the mind, especially as I looked after Mother, Lill, and Lallie and helped out with Mother-in-law Nellie who died at her daughter's home.

Fiona heard of my parting with Daisy and brought me flowers at teatime.

The cottage seemed quiet and lacking Daisy's presence – such a very good friend and very sadly missed, but I had to be grateful for the happiness we'd shared for fifteen years.

In the first week of January, I had a phone call from Chris Berry about an article in the Yorkshire Post's Saturday magazine "Country Week" as he wanted to enlarge on a letter I'd written to him about snowy winters in the past.

I spent some time looking through the old photo albums to find suitable illustrations, and added more details for the article.

Chris Berry and a photographer came early on January 9th and we got on well with many interests in common as he came from Hull too. The photographer just held his camera over photos still in the albums, and all so easy compared with the technique for my book illustrations. The photographer left when that job finished, but Chris and I talked for ages! Tony was so pleased to see the double spread in the Yorkshire Post supplement he phoned at 7.30 a.m.! We had a lot of interest in it from readers.

Later in the day, Pam phoned to say Richard Marshall had died in a car crash! Only 18 and driving back alone from a gamekeeper job interview with no other vehicle involved. We'd seen a lot of young Richard at Bygot with the Marshall family, and Robert a 'best friend' of Ian – such a sad waste of a young life! His funeral was especially sad, and Ian drove up to be with us in Etton church.

About that time too, the Revd. Derek Hodgson became ill – the start of a long illness and loss of interest in all his clerical duties, music and studying matters concerning ancient history and languages.

On Jan 13th I went to the pub here for a lunch with Ken Voase, Martin, Margo and Margo's mother Mona as it was Ken's birthday. They came back here for coffee and cake and I enjoyed their company till time to go with Jennifer and William to Malton.

William had an appointment before we were due at Rebecca's for a meal before seeing Sophie in the chorus of the Malton Pantomime. Rebecca and Geoff had seen other performances so we went to support Sophie that evening – and enjoyed the amateur production, which is well known for its high standard.

Sophie did well as one of the youngest dancers. I so loved being in dancing displays when her age.

Robert Peacock's funeral didn't take place until February 3rd when Jane Megginson called for me. We were directed to the front of the church! So many people we knew (old Malton Priory) and then on to Howe Bridge Farm which was overflowing with family and friends.

It was some time before I got a seat at Howe Bridge as so many there. We took Steve and Doreen home and also called on David Butterworth who had had a bad fall, but recovering. Janet, his daughter, was there and nice to see them.

I was always occupied with jobs in cottage or round village. I missed Daisy for walks, but on some dull wintry days was glad not to have to turn out and wrap up for a short walk before teatime. I wrote a lot of letters, and kept up my diary and went to meetings.

I seldom lit my fire till late afternoon, as kitchen warm with Aga and I liked the table for reading, writing or painting.

On 12th February, Jennifer and William gave a Sunday lunch for 14 'farming' guests – the chief entertainment being a film show! William had sorted out his Father's old cine films, and showed them in his 'office' room with chairs in rows.

They were of great interest, going back to early days of "tattying" even with gangs of hand pickers. The aerial crop spraying, primitive machinery and even the clothes worn were very different from to-day's obligatory boiler suits.

It was a very successful and happy gathering with lots to talk about.

For Maureen's 60th birthday in February, Barry had found a suitable house to rent for the week near Skipton. It was a lovely old house, stone and slate of typical Dales style set on a steep slope overlooking Lothersdale. We all enthused about the way it had been altered from a rather basic farmhouse to a "well appointed" and charming "family let".

I'm inclined to judge "good taste" by what I like and this was certainly "good taste" by my standards.

Barry and Maureen had had Lucy, Hannah and Colin at the weekend with Tony, Pam, Jane and children for an overnight stay. Then Colin went home, Sarah was there with Samuel and Jennifer, William and I arrived! William and Jennifer had the caravan and dogs as going on to the Lake District for two nights.

I stayed over the actual birthday, which was very lively with Dave bringing Alison and two more friends visiting for the evening meal, which Barry cooked in his usual brilliant way.

We also fitted in a morning in Skipton, and a visit to the owners nearby farm. The little ones were able to stroke calves, and to watch cows being milked by the latest methods, but I didn't feel it compared with the old ways of dairy cows deep in straw as in 'our' days. For one thing straw in the Dales has to be bought in from arable areas, and hosing down concrete is a quicker option!

On the Friday before we all left on the Saturday we had an interesting visit to Haworth and the Parsonage. A new experience for some of our party and I thought back to earlier visits with our young family, friends and even when buying a chest of drawers in an antique shop on the main street! I think we paid £15 and got it delivered to Cot Nab. Today, Tony and Pam use it and hopefully it has increased in value!

All together that Birthday week was a great success with another daughter becoming a Pensioner!

I did baking still in limited fashion, saw various friends, entertained some, and with either Nancie or Jennifer I went to see Susan English in the home at Bielby as often as we could as Susan seemed so pleased with visitors and village news.

I had a treat later in February when William and Jennifer took me with them for an overnight visit to see Ian in his Fenland cottage.

We arrived in time to have a packed lunch on his kitchen table. He had been working all the morning and no one at present sharing the cottage, which was basic, but adequate for farm workers or students.

Ian had made an effort to make it tidy and even found a tablecloth!

After lunch we were given a tour of the land near the cottage, taking Ian's dog as well as Jen's two for a pleasant walk near dykes and a man-made take. The weather was good and we also enjoyed being driven round the main farm about 12 miles away.

So many fields of vegetables and huge sheds, processing plants, machinery and lots of tractors! Also a lot of Eastern European workers.

Later we went to see our "B&B" near Wicken Fen, and found a lovely old house with very comfortable accommodation. We asked for advice about a place to eat in the evening and found the suggested ones were fully booked.

However, we got changed and tidied before collecting Ian who thought we could call at various pubs or restaurants he knew of. We tried three and then resorted to buying fish and chips in Soham and taking them to the cottage to eat there. With tea or coffee and cake we'd taken, it was a good meal, but no need to have changed our clothes.

The next morning, after an excellent breakfast, I was thrilled to visit Ely, as I'd always wanted to see this Fenland city, built on slightly elevated ground so long ago, and of course, the famous cathedral.

We only had a short time in which to look round the cathedral and to walk round the interesting streets near by in very cold weather. We were meeting Ian at Wicken Fen, not a really interesting place on a cold and dreary February morning, but we had hot drinks in the visitor centre, and I found a good birthday present for Great Grandson Edward, soon to have his 2nd birthday.

Ian took us to his favourite pub in Swaffham Prior where we had a good meal before saying 'goodbye' and setting off on the long, rather uninteresting drive home.

There was snow on the coast around Ash Wednesday when Jennifer and I went to the snowdrop garden at Hodsock Priory with other Garden Club members, all wrapped up well in the wintry weather. It was a beautiful garden, open only for snowdrops and winter flowering shrubs – during spring months. We had a long walk round and soup for lunch before driving back.

On my 87th birthday, I had gifts, flowers, callers and a meal at Skirpenbeck in the evening with Maureen, Mark and Lisa. Pam did well to cook it all, having been "riddling" tatties all day.

The previous day had been a celebration too, as Jennifer and I had lunch at the pub in Old Malton with Hilary Mason and daughter Suzanne from Farndale. We had so much to talk about I think the landlord thought we'd be there at teatime! However, Jennifer and I had time to shop in Malton and I chose a handbag as a present.

For many years I had suffered privately from a rectum prolapse! Not the sort of thing one talked about, and I think only Jack and my old friend Mickey knew of my trouble.

However in the last few years I found it very uncomfortable when walking, or even when working about the house. So I decided to do something about it in March, and to see a doctor in Pocklington. There are now nine doctors in the practice so one hardly knows any of them if lucky enough to have good health! So different from the old days when we knew our regular practitioner well and he would give a house call whenever needed! Also you could phone for advice if worried, and in the case of Maureen's sudden illness in early Cot Nab days, Dr. Isherwood even came out on Christmas Day!

Now all the local doctors have free weekends so try not to need to make emergency calls then or on Bank Holidays, because you only get in touch with a "duty doctor" who is probably miles away!

However, I was examined at the surgery in Pocklington for my unpleasant problem, and put on a list for a repair operation in York. True to present day National Health reputation my first notice from the Doctor was lost, so after enquiring as to a long delay in hearing anything, I did get an appointment to see a Mr Woodcock in the York Hospital. Jennifer took me there, and I felt so pleased to meet the very young and competent surgeon who made the somewhat embarrassing procedure quite easy.

I was then on a list for another more detailed exploration, again with Jennifer driving to and fro followed later by a date for the operation proceeded by an afternoon of tests to make sure I was fit enough!

Easter in 2006 proved quite eventful – we decorated the church as usual, and on Good Friday Ian went to the "Rugby Sevens" in Pocklington with Mark. To any one like me this seems a pointless event, other than officially to watch the rugby matches, it is evidently a long drinking session with a crowded bar in the marquee. It has a bad reputation in the town, as the day often ends with street fighting, and extra police are now drafted in to cope with all the mayhem.

Mark was sensible enough to phone Lisa to drive him home, and he suggested Ian went with them, but Ian decided to stay on, find his friend Kevin who has a house in Pocklington, but never found him. So when he went to his car later on, he was watched by two policemen who decided which of them should arrest him as they get points that way. If only they'd stopped him getting in the car, but no, they waited till he drove off – stopped and breathalysed him, and took him to a cell in Goole police station for the night!

The next morning he was driven back to Cot Nab and he continued to drive till his case was heard in Beverley.

On Easter Sunday, after early church, Ian drove me to Cayton where Maureen and Barry had a lovely party for the family. On the way there, Ian had lots to talk about, the farming in the Fens, and the difference from the Wolds. He was sorry about losing his licence, but admitted "It was the best night out I've ever had till I got caught".

The weather was warm enough to be out in the garden at Cayton with hidden eggs and other little gifts for Hannah to find and to give to all present.

After a good lunch we went to the sea, some in the car, and others walking with Samuel in the pushchair. Samuel was 'out of sorts' all day, crying a lot, even when pushed. Sarah was worried and had to drive to Strensall alone as David was working.

On the following Wednesday Maureen phoned early with the sad news that Samuel was in hospital with Meningitis!

We were all very worried and for Dave and Sarah a desperate week followed with ups and downs as the illness progressed. Sarah slept at the hospital, and Maureen visited with Barry. I'd told James straight away and on the Saturday he visited Sarah and Dave and prayed with them in spite of Dave being agnostic.

By the Monday Samuel was much better, but then got an infection, which delayed him going home. However, there were no after effects as often happens and he gradually returned to being his normal happy self.

That same week Nancie had a heart attack one night, and was in hospital two weeks! We were all worried, but she came through it all with little distress, and looking well! A warning though to be a little less active as she is a person always on the go and constantly helping others.

Ian managed to continue his life in the Fen country farming in spite of losing his driving licence for one year. His firm "Greens" was very helpful, arranging work to avoid driving on roads. Ian used his bike more, and had a good friend in Simon to drive him back to Harpers for exams necessary to qualify for the final year there which he managed to pass.

In the months before all this happened I had a visit by train to Wimbledon to spend two nights with Adrienne and Peter. A very pleasant little holiday, made very welcome as usual. I also enjoyed the taxi drives between Kings Cross and Wimbledon as much of interest to see on the way. Peter and Adrienne have led such extra interesting lives with distinguished careers – there is always much to talk about – also of our families.

In May I had a late birthday present from Maureen and Barry in the shape of an overnight hotel in London with tickets for the musical "Billy Elliott" which I longed to see, after enjoying the film.

Pam and Tony gave "pocket money" for this trip too, as there are always extra expenses, especially in London.

It was really a perfect two days after an early start, leaving for Strensall with Maureen after a night here. Sarah kindly drove us from Strensall after parking Maureen's car at their house, and with a quick train we were in London before midday.

A taxi to Victoria where the hotel was huge, modern and had a luxurious bedroom with all the "goodies" waiting for us. After lunch in the restaurant buffet we walked to Victoria coach station where nearby we could board the "Tour of London" bus as a way of seeing as much as possible without using too much energy for an "oldie" like me with a problem which luckily didn't cause too much bother!

Maureen enjoyed the tour on the top of the open bus as much as I did, and we even had a boat trip up the river from the Tower before changing to another bus.

We could, later on, walk the short distance from hotel to Victoria Palace and had a magical evening in a fully booked theatre with very enthusiastic audience. The boy playing "Billy" was the one from Hull, we thought must be the best of the four who alternated in the role, but I'm sure they were all wonderful in the lead part.

Before flopping into our beds we had some difficulty sorting our taps, shower and bath in the bathroom with too many mirrors for my liking! I had to fill the bath via the overhead shower and Maureen too had difficulties.

The next morning, we walked to Buckingham Palace to see the changing of the guard. Maureen had never watched this popular sight, and I not for many years. There were hundreds of tourists waiting with us.

I sat on the concrete base of the railings for part of the waiting time or chatted to two Americans who were spellbound by the entire spectacle. "We get nothing like this in the States". And later Mo was amused when the lady asked, "Is that your Mother? Isn't she cute"!

We were lucky to see the Household Cavalry passing by while exercising and also saw a visiting ambassador arriving by coach to present credentials, and driving through the archway. A sight, which intrigued the Americans even more.

At the end of this long ceremony I was ready to sit down! So we walked across to a bench in Green Park where we rested while licking ice cream cornets. Maureen had to buy another after hers came to grief on the floor to be enjoyed by a passing Labrador.

When I'd recovered my energy, our next stop was the Queen's gallery – disappointing except for luxury toilets, and then to the Royal Mews. This was another special treat, new to Maureen and I had only been in Coronation year!

We saw some of the "Windsor Greys", many different coaches with a good guide to explain all their uses before being amazed by the Golden State Coach, which only leaves the buildings every few years for extra special state occasions.

We also saw the Harness Room and Riding School before walking slowly back to the hotel to collect our luggage stopping for tea and cake on the way.

We eventually arrived back at Corner Cottage at 9 p.m. – After an especially enjoyable treat.

Elizabeth Brumfield had very bravely decided to have a quadruple by-pass operation in March with a pig's valve too, and got over it very well at 86, but it meant, of course, a long, slow and uncomfortable recovery. I visited with both Jennifer and Pam so we were all pleased when she was back home again.

Elizabeth's god-child Dianne was very good to her during this difficult time, and brought her to have lunch with me one sunny day – still looking frail, and not yet able to drive.

Our dear friend Jim Fitzpatrick had been in failing health at 92, for several months, getting gradually weaker and a great worry to Mary who coped valiantly, as not in the best of health herself. On May 24th we had the sad news of Jim's death. He had been in a Hospice for a short time, during which Mary had fallen in the house and broken her wrist badly.

On the last day of May (while Jennifer and William were in France) Tony and Pam collected Maureen and me by 7 a.m. as she had stayed overnight here, to drive to Jim's funeral in the church where I had attended services with them several times, as the Catholics shared the church with the Anglicans.

We were there early, and the weather perfect. A lovely meaningful service, and although I am not a 'grave' person I felt it right for Jim to be laid to rest in a corner of a country churchyard with the mountains all around, and blue skies beyond.

Poor Mary had the added trouble of her painful and useless wrist, but put on a brave face helped by family, and many good friends for a lunch in the pub nearby.

Afterwards we went to join the family at Hafan-y-Dorlan, and sat out on the patio with view of the river. It was good to talk to John, Steve, Anne, and to meet great-grandchild Mia before starting on the long journey home. When reminiscing about the old days Steve said he cried always on leaving Cot Nab!

It is hard to lose friends who have been close for so long, and to have shared with them joys and sometimes the sadness of family life.

I was worried too for Tom Sloan who had to leave his home in Gawsworth for long weeks in hospital before moving to a nursing home permanently.

On June 14th I gave a church lunch for four guests who paid £6 and then went on to invite three people! It could be a meal of any type. We found during the summer that some people entertained several friends, and then not all kept up the sequence.

By the end of the summer nearly £1,000 was raised, but few ended up asking two, and then one for coffee as originally planned.

There were some good Garden Club visits during the summer, and I enjoyed them all, but had to take my seat-stick to resort to using when my prolapse became difficult. Yet – one said nothing about such an unmentionable problem.

I did manage one morning to replace grubby old carpet in bathroom with a vinolay-looking-like-parquet flooring by laying the old carpet on top in the kitchen, cutting round, carrying upstairs and low and behold a smart new floor after a little extra trimming! I was pleased with the job and even Tony said it was O.K.

Our W.I. meeting in July took the form of a picnic at Pam's in Skirpenbeck. Lovely evening for weather, and the new garden was looking very good and flourishing.

We had a quiz, and a good supper though only sixteen of us as several on holiday.

A busy weekend started on Friday 14th preparing for my 'coffee morning and tea afternoon' in my cottage, courtyard and on the gravel space at the back.

We were lucky with a warm, sunny day and set out stalls in the garage with Tombola on the gravel with chairs, tables and benches.

I had lots of good helpers, and William brought trestle tables, a big umbrella, and extra chairs.

Jennifer helped all day in the kitchen, as well as Elizabeth, Nancie and others. We had a Traidcraft stall too and used their tea, coffee and biscuits.

A lot of people came in the morning with not as many in the afternoon, but they enjoyed sitting out, and having tea and newly made scones which Jennifer and Sandra baked in the lunch break.

I was tired by the end of the day, in spite of sitting down when possible. We made £350 for St. Edith's and £130 for Traidcraft.

The next day, Sunday was the annual family picnic. Again in the spell of hot dry weather. I went with Jennifer and William after church to find a good number already established in the off road paddock at Levisham with gazebos and umbrellas set up as usual.

About eight were missing in the family, but nice to have Alison with new partner Des. We walked to the station as usual, and I enjoyed the art exhibition where I met the artist whose family came from Bolton near us and I even talked to his mother who remembered me giving a talk to the Fangfoss W.I.

The following week on the Monday July 24th I went into York Hospital by the Medibus, which collected me at the door, rather late, but being 'admitted' that afternoon the time wasn't important.

I was in a ward with four other ladies, all pleasant, but suffered disastrous results that evening after being given a drink to empty my bowels! There should have been another dose, but when the nurse was called to deal with the violent effects of the first one, she reported, "The doctor says, no need for any more medication!"

I had the operation early the next morning, the first ever for me, and I found it all quite interesting and no real discomfort, other than nausea in the afternoon.

Grandchildren, Alison, Sarah and Jane visited during the three days I was in the hospital, and Pam came to drive me home. I'd been so grateful to Mr Woodcock for dealing with the operation. He'd told me it had taken an hour and quite a big length removed from the bowel, so I mustn't do heavy lifting for a time.

I felt really well, if rather feeble and as Pam had to go back to land work and Jennifer away, it was nice to see Lucy who drove over from Harrogate leaving Hannah with her Daddy. Lucy was very large 'with child' and had made me a cake. I was delighted to see her and to have the cake and appreciated her effort in coming.

Maureen came after work and stayed overnight, but I was able to look after myself as usual.

Jennifer was back the next day and I progressed well, till ready to pack for the Scarborough holiday with the family after a week of getting stronger, able to go to the shop, have a hair trim in Pocklington and even a Sunday in the garden at Cayton when Maureen and Barry had one of their

Sunday walks for friends with lots of food served too.

The hot weather continued for the Scarborough week in a specially comfortable and interesting house with garden overlooking Peasholm Park.

The children, Thomas, Jack, Sophie, Cameron and baby Eva were all very happy and we had days on different beaches with visiting family too.

Tony came one evening after going to York for back treatment, Maureen and Barry called in after a long Sunday walk, and Pam came with Jane and her children Laura and Edward staying on for an evening meal when there were fifteen to feed.

On the Sunday before that Christopher came over with Nicola, driven by friend Gordon, but they spent the day in the bathing pool before joining us for supper.

The week passed all too quickly and I loved it all, only on the last day was there a change in the weather and rain 'set in' for the rest of August, causing delays and frustrations for combining.

It was lovely to have Mary Fitzpatrick here (by taxi) on August 21st, Tony and Pam came here for supper - Mary stayed for a few days. The weather wasn't too bad, and nearly all the family managed to see us. Rebecca kindly took us to see Lucy and Sally with their new baby girls! Lucy had had Freya while we were in Scarborough and Sally produced Rachel the following week.

So we had a pleasant day visiting the two families in Harrogate and Knaresborough, after an early lunch here in the cottage.

We met up with others in the family at Jennifer's as she was busy having grandchildren to stay and we also had a meal at the pub here with Jane and her two, and Sarah with Samuel.

Mary and I had lots to talk about, and I'm sure the change did her good, it being the first little holiday without dear Jim.

There had been difficulties with William's Mother, Mary Foster, aged 96, since she collapsed in her bedroom on William's 65th birthday.

Jennifer had prepared a special lunch, and Mary had felt well enough to say she would attend service at Kirby Underdale church first – so Jennifer and I left William in church, before going to collect Mary.

There followed quite a dramatic day as no sign of Mary when we arrived at Birks Farm, which stands alone down a drive off the Buttercrambe-Stamford Bridge road.

There was no answer to the phone, door locked and nothing to see through downstairs windows. So after phoning Fordham to ask someone to get William out of church, Jennifer decided to climb through the pantry window!

We broke off the wire mesh to find it unlocked, so with a stool to stand on Jen climbed through on to a table and I followed saying "I'm coming too!"

We climbed the stairs calling "Hallo" and were so relieved to hear a faint reply.

Poor Mary was lying on the floor midst confusion in her bedroom with upturned table, phone hanging loose, and bed clothes in a heap, but she could talk to us and didn't seem in pain.

After covering her up as she was only wearing a vest, I stayed upstairs, while Jen went to phone for an ambulance (no local doctors on duty at weekends!) and to meet William who had been brought with Alison Foster and the boys!

The ambulance men were kind and efficient, but decided no need to take Mary to hospital as all she needed was sleep in bed!

What about the birthday lunch? Jennifer and William went back to Limetree House, to rescue it, and to bring it to Birks with the birthday cake, and also William's overnight things!

So it was late when we ate stuffed pork etc at the kitchen table with William's son Richard, wife and two children being re-routed to come for tea and cake later, also bringing presents.

Anne-Marie being a nurse reassured us about Mary who stayed in bed, and we sang "Happy Birthday" with Lizzie and Patrick. What a day!

So William became nurse and housekeeper for Mary, and organised a bed downstairs for her, but after a few weeks they all decided that Mary should move to Limetree.

This move has made life easier than trying to keep Birks going too and Mary has the far sitting room as her bedroom, spending quite a lot of time lying on the bed.

She can walk round downstairs, has meals in the dining room, and has started knitting squares again. Her short sight is bad, but she still watches "Countdown" and instructs William in baking fruit loaves and Christmas cakes.

Luckily through Maureen they found Anne Early to be a house sitter and carer if they want a holiday or long days out.

Mary has improved a lot in recent weeks and I can 'pop in' if necessary or have had her brought here for lunch – once with Anne to drive her round and another day with daughter Ruth.

I still ask Ken Voase to lunch about once in three weeks and enjoyed the conversation, getting up to date with family and farming news.

Once he had a quick lunch here one day earlier in the month and then took me to Baswick to look round the farm in general. It was lovely weather with his family busy with harvest on the low lying good land beside the river Hull, which grows extra good wheat. There were also beautiful blue fields of borage, and a drive all around the woodland where fruit trees on the edge of the plantation showed promise of rich pickings later.

Ken had planted trees in great numbers and in many varieties in early married life – a wonderful idea, as fifty years later they have added both interest, beauty and good wind breaks around the fields.

After meeting some of the family and inspecting workshops, corn store and garden we had tea in the kitchen where Ken managed well – pushing a chair around laden with things he couldn't carry.

Later Ken's daughter Heather kindly drove me home, going out of the way to show me a luxury development of "executive type" houses in the grounds of Brandesburton Hall, no longer used as a hospital for mental patients. With flats and staff accommodation now changed to up-market residences. I was truly amazed by the number of "posh" homes, and wondered at the change in rural living with the large detached dwellings in "tasteful" surroundings, ornate embellishments, often looking as if having five bedrooms (no doubt all with "en-suite") and not too large a garden as is the general requirement of modern villagers in the 21st century!

September 15th was a memorable occasion as Lord and Lady Halifax entertained tenants and families to a reception celebrating the forth-coming marriage of Lord Irwin to Georgia Clarkson.

A minibus awaited us at Bishop Wilton bridge, and I walked down with William and Jennifer in our best outfits to join others. There were similar services made for other estate villages including Heslington and from Hickleton.

The weather was perfect and driving though the park to the Hall is a treat in itself. We 'unloaded' through the courtyard, so walked along the terrace where musicians played and guests strolled in evening dress to meet Lord Irwin and his future bride before going into the Hall where we were free to wander, to meet friends, to chat, drink champagne or other choice of wines, and to nibble extra good canapés.

Lord Halifax walked round the various rooms encouraging us to eat "as this is your first course".

Garrowby, rebuilt for the present Earl, except for the library and chapel, is a delightful place – feeling very much a lived in home, although filled with priceless treasures, pictures and photographs.

There were elaborate tented enclosures in the courtyard and a vast marquee where the numerous tables were set out for dinner. I found my table easily, and Lady Susan was the family representative, and Jack and I had known her for many years through fund raising for the Middleton Hunt and in the Pony Club years.

Jennifer and William felt honoured to be at Lord Irwin's table, and Jennifer found him easy to talk to, and Georgia proved to be a delightful girl.

I sat next to Steve Megginson, so plenty of conversation! The food was tender lamb with roast vegetables and the pudding a rich chocolate concoction known as "Eton Mess" on the menu, and containing much cream and strawberries.

It was a lovely idea for Kit Jackson to propose Lord Irwin's health. Kit is the housekeeper and has worked hard for the family over many years, since her son and James Irwin spent boyhood years together in the Park - with amusing escapades referred to in her speech. Kit is married to Tim, the son of Jack's cousin Barbara and Tim is also valuable help on the Estate and in the Hall.

The whole evening was friendly with great hospitality. Pam and Tony were at Lady Caroline's table and knew people to talk to. Lady Caroline is also a sister of Lord Halifax and since her marriage has lived mostly in Devon. Always sounding so pleased to be up here again and meeting estate people.

We were ferried home at 11.30, having been delayed by the late arrival to the bus by Rector James and Harold Carr, the retired head gamekeeper! Both men enjoy their drink and James's excuse was looking after, and waiting for Harold!

I was tired as I got into bed, but so thrilled to have been invited to yet another Garrowby celebration, a tradition in that eminent family!

Incidentally the 'loos' were part of Tony and Mark's business, and the next day Pam was on duty as a cleaner as the toilets had to be in use again on the Sunday for a family lunch.

After a lapse of about a year in requests for giving talks, I had three in September! I really enjoyed all three, two to "Countrywomen" in Melbourne and Wetwang, and the other to a luncheon club near Market Weighton.

I was fortunate that on each occasion, a driver was arranged for me, so I had the added pleasure of meeting two old friends, and new ones, as well as renewing acquaintances in the audiences.

Ian, now 21, had been back at Cot Nab for two weeks, mostly spent ploughing, before going back to Harper Adams for his final year.

As Ian was still unable to drive, Tony had valiantly driven very early down to the cottage on the Fens to collect all the stuff acquired over the last year. Dog with kennel, computer, fridge and goodness knows what else and it all took a lot of loading. They were back by midday, so Jennifer and I went up to see him briefly, and to give him the warm jacket bought for his birthday by Jennifer, Maureen and me. It fitted well, and he was obviously delighted to have it. He had decided to celebrate his birthday later by bringing four other student friends to Cot Nab for a weekend and to go to York Races, as well as showing them the wold countryside.

As others were busy combining William kindly drove Ian back to Harpers for the new term, going there and back in a day.

I didn't see Ian or his friends, but heard it all went off well with help in entertaining from Lisa and Mark.

On another weekend Ian was driven up by his friend Simon, and this time I met them both at a good and lively meal at Skirpenbeck. They had again had a good 'night out' in York, but we didn't hear any details, perhaps as well.

Curly and Jane's children, Laura and Edward, were at Skirpenbeck that day too and are a lot of fun. Tony recently laid low with his recurring bad back trouble was recovering enough to play with them round garden and house with many shrieks of joy from the lively pair.

Jennifer and William were away that week, so missed seeing Ian.

Anne Early, Mary's 'sitter', has led an interesting life, and we have quite a lot in common as she also started life in Hull, in Newland Park, and the Avenues, and even went to the French Convent for four years and her mother had also been a pupil!

Maureen was now reaching the end of her years at "Take it Easy" in Pocklington as now a 'Pensioner' and feeling ready to literally "take it easy". She had made many friends in this job, starting with her boss, Maggie, and husband, and got on well with the seemingly hundreds of clients whom I'm sure would be missed, as she would by them.

I would miss her late night working on Thursdays when she'd been a weekly "supper, bed and breakfast" visitor – often Tony would call round to see her here, and Jennifer popped in too either during the evening or to chat over breakfast.

It meant a long day's work for Maureen, with the drive to and fro from Cayton, and I'm sure it will be much easier with more free time to spend at home with Barry, to go for walks and not to be up by the alarm clock each morning, especially in the dark days of winter with road problems in frosty weather.

Dear old Coidy had been failing in health for some time, and soon after her 97th birthday she spent weeks in hospital before dying on October 27th. I shall miss her so much as the most lively personality who has been part of all our lives for so long, and going back to early Fraisthorpe years. She was still president of the English Speaking Board when she died, using her secretary Pauline weekly. Pauline had taken over even helping with personal letters like mine, since Coidy's sight became so bad. Her companion, partner (when in the Southport Drama school years) Jocelyn Bell has been a dear friend for so long, and will find life very strange (and quiet) without the vibrant Christobel.

Also around this October time the Reverend Derek Hodgson had become so ill and mentally affected that he had spent some weeks in a nursing home, after months in hospital.

It has been a difficult time, and Derek had been such a help to James Finnemore, not only in helping with sermons, but playing the organ and generally becoming part of the village since retiring from Mytholmroyd.

Derek died on October 12th, even more sadly this happened as Elizabeth Hodgson came out of York Hospital after a gall bladder operation – so a very difficult week followed, but the funeral went off very well with a full church. Jennifer had helped with flowers, as Elizabeth still too weak. Luckily her old friend Gwen came to stay from Watford and made things easier.

Yet another Church Bazaar is planned. I think back to all the November weeks in other years since we came to Bishop Wilton parish, and of the variety of things I made during dark evenings by the fire. There were hobbyhorses, note pads, peg dolls, pencils topped by heads made from ping-pong balls when grandchildren helped.

Yards of fur fabric were turned into door-dogs, which also sold well, as did the hobbyhorses. Jack, of course, was a big help with those, fixing on the broom handles, and seeing to the bridles. He didn't like using fabric instead of leather for this, but over the years we took short cuts and had less patience.

On November 15th Lorna Sleightholme died. Poor Lorna had had cancer and diabetes for the last year, but her life was quite full in spite of needing carers in the mornings, and help from her nearby family too. Lorna had always been a warm hearted lady who loved people, had countless friends and had mixed well, so during her illness there were many afternoon callers to cheer her up. She had also been well enough for car drives out till within two weeks of her death.

Having been born in Bishop Wilton and married to a local farmer Bob, they had both joined in so many activities and societies, leading very full lives. I've written of Bob and Lorna before as Jack and I had many shared pleasures together.

Lorna had played the church organ regularly since the age of fifteen, and was sad to give it up when her hands became stiff a few years ago. On November 24th there was a very good service and overflowing church for Lorna's funeral.

With so many friends dying in the last years, I have felt big gaps in my life and our old friend Joan Atkinson is another who meant a lot to us. Peter was a cousin of Jack's, and through his recommendation we got the tenancy of Cot Nab.

I shall finish this book before Christmas 2006 to avoid more repetition much the same as other years.

I think very much of the changes in my long life and of farming methods undreamed of when I first met Jack. I think it important to record these changes and hope my books have helped readers to understand about a life-style, which will soon be forgotten.

The fact that Cot Nab has no stock of any kind belonging to the Megginsons is strange enough, but who would have thought of luxury mobile toilets becoming a diversification? As lack of farming profits made it harder to make a living, many farmers decided to find extra ways of making a better living. Tony and Mark decided a few years ago to buy two toilet units from the Convenience Company and since then they have expanded to have six in their 'fleet'.

Painted dark green, they have carpets, the up-market fixtures necessary to impress and even the odd flower vase and picture.

Keeping up a high standard is hard work and Pam is the 'cleaner-in-chief'!

Tony, Mark, Curly Cartledge at times and occasional extra drivers take the toilets behind Land Rover Discoveries up and down all parts of the North East. They visit interesting places, meet clients and on the whole seem to enjoy the work.

Lisa is head of the office part with organisation, dealing with orders, computer work and advertising. Lisa and Pam can drive, but 'setting up' isn't always easy if the site is uneven and the steps have to be put in place, a skirt round the base and electricity and water connected. The 'effluent' is discharged to a holding tank at Cot Nab and finally disposed of by a waste disposal company.

Sometimes a unit is required over two or three days for corporate entertaining so someone has to go to check on them and supply more water.

Marquee firms give orders and it is a bonus to have race meeting contracts.

The winter months are slack naturally though Christmas time may bring in orders. I think Jack would have been very surprised by the demand for such things! As I look back and Christmas draws near I feel we have gone too far in materialism with too much expected from life. It was easier in some ways to just have a two-day Christmas and no holiday over New Year.

Now it lasts so long, there are people who get to the 'fed up' (yes literally) stage and frustrated, exhausted and often penniless as shops seldom close and the media puts pressure on us all with much 'plastic' used to purchase goods often just luxuries.

I still enjoy my life, find great interest in all the changes and above all, that which goes on in my still increasing family. I'm so thankful to have good sight and am an avid reader. My memory is good, and most of my memories are good. Having known hard work I can appreciate the benefits of modern living, but regret the passing of many of the standards of good behaviour. Today 'anything goes' and there is little alternative to go along with it while trying to stick to some principles which are often ignored.

At least, having written down my thoughts and my history my children will know more about their parents and forbears than I did about mine! I was kept in the dark mostly as was the trend in those far off days. Now there are few secrets and perhaps the world is better for it.

One remarkable thing is the fact that this book, like my others, has been written by hand using a "Biro" pen. This type of pen was invented around the time of my thirtieth birthday when Joan gave me one as a present. They were quite expensive at first, but a great boon after fountain pens of which I'd used a variety, Waterman, Conway Stewart and a good Parker! The last an unexpected gift from Jack.

To-day e-mails replace letters and the young particularly all use text messages on their mobile phones, so one doesn't need to even spell correctly!

Modern technology is a mystery to me, but it's essential for even the very young.

We spent little time in our cold bedrooms, but now it is normal for schoolchildren to have computers and TV's in bedrooms, which are seldom shared with brothers and sisters.

Medical science has progressed to the pitch when the Health Service is over-stretched in all departments.

In the 'old days' when medical help had to be paid for by one and all, people in general only called in a doctor when situations bordered on becoming serious and then a 'home call' was normal. Medical and dental bills were a great worry to lower income groups.

Our home made remedies sufficed and so different from the practise of visiting the surgery for any little ailment which results in more patients than even our nine GP's can comfortably cope with and at weekends only an emergency doctor is available.

It was much easier, of course, when village parishes had one clergyman to themselves! We even had one who didn't drive and now we are part of a benefice of five!

I feel schools too have far too many pupils at the secondary stage with well over a thousand in most state schools, and so much pressure put on students to pass exams, go to Universities where even good degrees can result in difficulties in getting the jobs they deserve.

With all the horrors facing the youth of to-day, drug addition, alcoholism, sex from an early age and less discipline in families, I feel life is becoming more and more difficult to face up to, but throughout history there has always been change and progression, so I can only hope and pray for my family in the future!

View up village from Corner Cottage (Photo Mike Pratt)

Irene with friend Nancie outside Corner Cottage with Daisy

Ian in my sitting room, aged 17, walks to visit Gran

Tom Sloan in courtyard, Corner Cottage

'Old Girls' Mickey, Adrienne and Oxo at the Jackson's Wimbledon flat

Tony, Irene & others at Corner Cottage kitchen during Christmas party

Irene - bathes

POST SCRIPTUM – JULY 2007

I can't let this book get into print without adding a few more thoughts and ideas as life moves on. First the great grandchildren now number eleven with Christopher the eldest at 19 and the youngest Luke aged four months. As far as we know, no more due this year! Ian, my youngest grandchild, is due to leave college and plans four months farm work in New Zealand. There is also the good news that Mark and Lisa plan a wedding in March 2008.

I'm still amazed by the cost of bringing up families in these more prosperous days of unlimited supplies of baby amusements. Varied wardrobes of designer outfits and endless bright plastic things that swing, bleep or produce cheerful and continuous tunes!

Our children would be considered deprived if compared with modern families, but did it do them harm to be less pandered to, less stimulated and when formal education didn't involve being pushed into passing endless exams?

Plus no technology – if any of my great grandchildren ever read this book it will seem like the dark ages, as I manage with neither computer, CD's, mobile phone, microwave oven nor dishwasher. As time marches on I expect many more such high-tech inventions will flood the market. Will people read books or write letters with pen and paper?

Even now some young children become adults before their 'teens. Childhood games relying on imagination, with items for play being home produced are becoming obsolete.

Marriages generally don't last as long – I remember Mabel Barmby who helped me in the house at Fraisthorpe talking of a forthcoming village marriage with the remark "Well there's more as sticks it, as doesn't!" True sixty years ago, but now it isn't necessary to "stick it" at all, if it doesn't suit.

I'm quite happy to have old time recollections while sitting back to ɔy a family picnic, seaside holiday or to visit mums with babies, and to ᵓused by the toddlers. How Jack would have loved these newcomers ʲamily! And they in turn would have loved him.